Guide for Discipling

Experiencing God
Spiritual Responsiveness
Sacrificial Service
Generous Living
Disciplemaking
Personal Transformation
Authentic Relationships
Community Transformation

Robert E. Logan
with Charles R. Ridley

A Discipleship Difference Resource

Published by Logan Leadership

Visit us at http://loganleadership.com

ISBN 978-1-944955-38-0

Acknowledgement

Tara Miller's exceptional writing skills bring our thoughts and ideas to life. Above all others, she makes this book possible. Over many years, her creative collaboration makes it possible to give written resources to the Church so that people can discover and live out their God-given purpose.

Contents

Acknowledgement   3

The Dimensions of Discipleship   7

Experiencing God   15

   I. Increasing your awareness of God's love and presence   17
   II. Growing in the knowledge and grace of God   23
   III. Reflecting on and applying scripture in your everyday life   29
   IV. Dialoguing authentically with God   35
   V. Worshipping God in spirit and in truth   41

Spiritual Responsiveness   47

   I. Receiving guidance and empowerment from the Holy Spirit   49
   II. Discerning opportunities for involvement in God's work   55
   III. Checking what you're hearing with scripture and your faith community   61
   IV. Acting in faith through loving obedience   65
   V. Listening for God's calling in your life   71

Sacrificial Service   77

   I. Blessing others with your words and deeds   79
   II. Partnering with others to minister in practical ways   83
   III. Ministering personally and appropriately to the poor   87
   IV. Speaking up for people experiencing injustice   93
   V. Cultivating a compassionate heart   99

Generous Living   103

   I. Managing your time and resources for kingdom purposes   105
   II. Using your spiritual gifts to bless others   111
   III. Giving your money generously and wisely   117
   IV. Showing hospitality without favoritism   121
   V. Living out your God-given calling   127

Disciplemaking — 131

I. Engaging in spiritual conversations with those who are not yet followers of Jesus — 133
II. Explaining the good news and the way of Jesus — 139
III. Establishing new believers in a discipleship process — 145
IV. Connecting people with a faith community — 151
V. Helping new followers make more followers — 155

Personal Transformation — 161

I. Actively engaging with God in the examination of your heart — 163
II. Cooperating with God's healing work in your life — 169
III. Processing feedback and input from others — 175
IV. Living out new priorities and changed behavior — 179
V. Increasingly bearing the fruit of the Spirit — 185

Authentic Relationships — 191

I. Showing respect for all people — 193
II. Forgiving others and asking forgiveness — 199
III. Confronting each other with humility when necessary — 205
IV. Praying for and with others — 211
V. Supporting each other honestly through life challenges — 217

Community Transformation — 221

I. Participating in a faith community that reaches outside of itself — 223
II. Praying for healing and reconciliation in society — 229
III. Involving yourself in social justice needs in the broader community — 235
IV. Caring for God's creation in practical ways — 241
V. Helping others create healthy lives and relationships — 247
What's next? — 251
About the Authors — 253
About Logan Leadership — 253
Appendix — 255

Introduction

The Dimensions of Discipleship

Love God. Love People. Make Disciples.

A disciple of Jesus is a reflection of God in the world. When Jesus talked about discipleship, it was an all-in kind of thing.

> A large crowd was following Jesus. He turned around and said to them, 26 "If you want to be my disciple, you must, by comparison, hate everyone else—your father and mother, wife and children, brothers and sisters—yes, even your own life. Otherwise, you cannot be my disciple. 27 And if you do not carry your own cross and follow me, you cannot be my disciple.
>
> 28 "But don't begin until you count the cost. For who would begin construction of a building without first calculating the cost to see if there is enough money to finish it? 29 Otherwise, you might complete only the foundation before running out of money, and then everyone would laugh at you. 30 They would say, 'There's the person who started that building and couldn't afford to finish it!'"
> — Luke 14:25-30

We don't have to be perfect to be Jesus' disciples, but we do have to know what we are signing up for and be willing to submit all areas of life to God. As Jesus discipled people, he expected that their discipleship would touch all aspects of their life, relationships, and even society as a whole.

A real disciple needs to embrace and be growing in all the dimensions of discipleship. We can't be ¾ of a disciple, picking and choosing, for a disciple when fully trained is like his or her teacher: Jesus (Luke 6:40). True discipleship is holistic: we can't be content to be growing in some areas and lacking in other areas.

As we've considered the nature of discipleship, we've created a diagram to represent the 8 dimensions of a disciple. As Jesus became incarnate and lived among us, these are the ways we see him living. Take a look at the diagram and categories that follow. Examine it to see how the pieces fit together. Then evaluate your own life. Allow others to speak into your life as well: we never travel alone on the journey of allowing God to work in our lives.

Here are the eight dimensions of a disciple of Jesus:

- **Experiencing God**
- **Spiritual Responsiveness**
- **Sacrificial Service**
- **Generous Living**

- **Disciplemaking**
- **Personal Transformation**
- **Authentic Relationships**
- **Community Transformation**

Experiencing God: Intentionally and consistently engaging with God in such a way that you open yourself to a deeper understanding of him and deeper relationship with him.

Supporting Scriptures:

He answered, "'Love the Lord your God with all your heart and with all your soul and with all your strength and with all your mind'; and, 'Love your neighbor as yourself.'" — Luke 10:27

Behavioral Expressions:

- **Increasing your awareness of God's love and presence**
- **Growing in the knowledge and grace of God**
- **Reflecting on and applying scripture in your everyday life**
- **Dialoguing authentically with God**
- **Worshipping God in spirit and in truth**

Spiritual Responsiveness: Actively listening to the Holy Spirit and taking action according to what you are hearing.

Supporting Scriptures:

Since we are living by the Spirit, let us follow the Spirit's leading in every part of our lives. — Galatians 5:25

Trust in the Lord with all your heart; do not depend on your own understanding. Seek his will in all you do, and he will show you which path to take. — Proverbs 3:5-6

Do not merely listen to the word, and so deceive yourselves. Do what it says. — James 1:22

Behavioral Expressions:

- **Receiving guidance and empowerment from the Holy Spirit**
- **Discerning opportunities for involvement in God's work**
- **Checking what you're hearing with scripture and your faith community**
- **Acting in faith through loving obedience**
- **Listening for God's calling in your life**

Sacrificial Service: Doing good works even when it's costly, inconvenient or challenging.

Supporting Scriptures:

For we are God's masterpiece. He has created us anew in Christ Jesus, so we can do the good things he planned for us long ago. — Ephesians 2:10

Their only suggestion was that we keep on helping the poor, which I have always been eager to do. — Galatians 2:10

Behavioral Expressions:

- **Blessing others with your words and deeds**

- **Partnering with others to minister in practical ways**

- **Ministering personally and appropriately to the poor**

- **Speaking up for people experiencing injustice**

- **Cultivating a compassionate heart**

Generous Living: Faithfully stewarding what God has given you so you can contribute toward the advancement of the Kingdom.

Supporting Scriptures:

"Again, the Kingdom of Heaven can be illustrated by the story of a man going on a long trip. He called together his servants and entrusted his money to them while he was gone. He gave five bags of silver to one, two bags of silver to another, and one bag of silver to the last—dividing it in proportion to their abilities. He then left on his trip...." — Matthew 25:14-15

"If you are faithful in little things, you will be faithful in large ones. But if you are dishonest in little things, you won't be honest with greater responsibilities." — Luke 16:10

Behavioral Expressions:

- **Managing your time and resources for kingdom purposes**

- **Using your spiritual gifts to bless others**

- **Giving your money generously and wisely**

- **Showing hospitality without favoritism**

- **Living out your God-given calling**

Introduction

Disciplemaking: Living in obedience to the great commission given by Jesus, which entails making more and better followers of Christ.

Supporting Scriptures:

> *"Therefore, go and make disciples of all the nations, baptizing them in the name of the Father and the Son and the Holy Spirit. Teach these new disciples to obey all the commands I have given you. And be sure of this: I am with you always, even to the end of the age." — Matthew 28:19-20*

Behavioral Expressions:

- **Engaging in spiritual conversations with those who are not yet followers of Jesus**

- **Explaining the good news and the way of Jesus**

- **Establishing new believers in a discipleship process**

- **Connecting people with a faith community**

- **Helping new followers make more followers**

Personal Transformation: Changing your attitudes and behaviors in positive ways as a result of your relationship with God and others.

Supporting Scripture:

> *Don't copy the behavior and customs of this world, but let God transform you into a new person by changing the way you think. Then you will learn to know God's will for you, which is good and pleasing and perfect. — Romans 12:2*

Behavioral Expressions:

- **Actively engaging with God in the examination of your heart**

- **Cooperating with God's healing work in your life**

- **Processing feedback and input from others**

- **Living out new priorities and changed behavior**

- **Increasingly bearing the fruit of the Spirit**

Authentic Relationships: Engaging with other people in ways that reflect the heart of God toward them.

Supporting Scripture:

"Do to others whatever you would like them to do to you. This is the essence of all that is taught in the law and the prophets." — Matthew 7:12

Behavioral Expressions:

- **Showing respect for all people**
- **Forgiving others and asking forgiveness**
- **Confronting others with humility as necessary**
- **Praying with and for others**
- **Supporting each other honestly through life challenges**

Community Transformation: Personal involvement with others to facilitate positive change where you live and beyond

Supporting Scripture:

And the one sitting on the throne said, "Look, I am making everything new!" —Revelation 21:5a

Now all glory to God, who is able, through his mighty power at work within us, to accomplish infinitely more than we might ask or think. Glory to him in the church and in Christ Jesus through all generations forever and ever! Amen. — Ephesians 3:20-21

Behavioral Expressions:

- **Participating in a faith community that reaches outside of itself**
- **Praying for healing and reconciliation in society**
- **Involving yourself in social justice needs in the broader community**
- **Caring for God's creation in practical ways**
- **Helping others cultivate healthy lives and relationships**

How to use the guides

The eight topics just described flow from our previous book, The Discipleship Difference: Making disciples while growing as disciples. The book lays out our full philosophy of making disciples. This set of 8 discipleship guides then is essentially an expansion of chapter two, where we discuss the qualities of a disciple. What is a disciple? How would you know if you saw one? What behaviors would he or she exhibit? You can then use these guides to grow in holistic discipleship.

The guides that follow are organized according to the tree diagram above. Experiencing God, at the root of the tree, focuses on the way we interact and dialogue with God, the way we become increasingly aware of his presence, and how we continue to form a more personal relationship with him. This root is necessary for all of the other areas, as they flow out of our experience of God.

Spiritual Responsiveness then builds on those roots as we seek to listen to God and respond to the voice of his Spirit in obedience. From there, the branches can be worked through in any order, according to what you are hearing from God.

The end result will be transformation-- not of ourselves only-- but of others and the whole of the community around us.

You can use these guides in a variety of ways. Meet together in small groups, or better yet, groups of three or four. When you meet, open by following up on your most recent time together. Ask each other these questions:

- **What are you especially thankful for since we last gathered?**
- **What are your current challenges?**
- **How can we be helpful?**
- **With whom did you share your learnings from our last time together?**
- **How did it go with your action items from last time?**

Then dive into the material for this week. Read scripture passages and ask one another the questions. Wait for and listen to responses from the heart. Encourage, challenge, and affirm one another.

Allow time for connection and prayer at the end of your gathering. There is great value in doing life together and consistently praying for one another.

You can also use these guides one-on-one in your discipling relationships. However you choose to go through them, go at your own pace: you can do one a week or one a month, whatever pace works best for you. Be sure to allow enough time to live into these behaviors, because next time you meet you'll begin by asking each other the same follow up questions about your action items.

Experiencing God

Intentionally and consistently engaging with God in such a way that you open yourself to a deeper understanding of him and deeper relationship with him

I. Increasing your awareness of God's love and presence

Key question: *How are you intentionally becoming more aware of God's presence and his love for you?*

Sometimes we feel a sense of God's presence on an emotional level and sometimes we don't. We know he is always there, regardless of how we feel. How can we connect to the love and presence of God even when he feels far away from us? The presence of God is what sustains and nourishes us when we have trouble or when difficult journeys are ahead of us.

Sometimes we sense his love and presence in the big things—the major changes and challenges in our lives—and sometimes we sense his love and presence in the small things—a gentle breeze or the sun on our face. Our goal in increasing our awareness of God's love and presence is not manufacturing emotion, but getting in touch with how God is already speaking to us and then recognizing his presence in our lives.

 Meditation

> Bede Griffiths, a Benedictine monk, details something he experienced as a boy. He was walking in the evening when he was suddenly dazzled by the beautiful song of a flock of birds. The beauty of their singing seemed to awaken senses he'd never used before. In an instant the world seemed magically transformed, and everything in it seemed to burst with what he calls a "kind of sacramental character. I remember now the feeling of awe which came over me," he wrote, "I felt inclined to kneel on the ground... and I hardly dared to look on the face of the sky, because it seemed as though it was but a veil before the face of God."
>
> When have you experienced something like this? Take time to re-imagine that time in your mind, re-creating the sensory experience.

This week read and reflect daily on the scripture on the next page. Open a natural flow of conversational prayer with the Holy Spirit as you meditate on the scriptures, inviting him to reveal himself to you. Then gather with those who journey alongside you and interact over the discipleship questions.

1 Kings 19:3-18

Elijah was afraid and fled for his life. He went to Beersheba, a town in Judah, and he left his servant there. 4 Then he went on alone into the wilderness, traveling all day. He sat down under a solitary broom tree and prayed that he might die.

"I have had enough, Lord," he said. "Take my life, for I am no better than my ancestors who have already died."

5 Then he lay down and slept under the broom tree. But as he was sleeping, an angel touched him and told him, "Get up and eat!" 6 He looked around and there beside his head was some bread baked on hot stones and a jar of water! So he ate and drank and lay down again.

7 Then the angel of the Lord came again and touched him and said, "Get up and eat some more, or the journey ahead will be too much for you."

8 So he got up and ate and drank, and the food gave him enough strength to travel forty days and forty nights to Mount Sinai, the mountain of God. 9 There he came to a cave, where he spent the night.

But the Lord said to him, "What are you doing here, Elijah?"

10 Elijah replied, "I have zealously served the Lord God Almighty. But the people of Israel have broken their covenant with you, torn down your altars, and killed every one of your prophets. I am the only one left, and now they are trying to kill me, too."

11 "Go out and stand before me on the mountain," the Lord told him. And as Elijah stood there, the Lord passed by, and a mighty windstorm hit the mountain. It was such a terrible blast that the rocks were torn loose, but the Lord was not in the wind. After the wind there was an earthquake, but the Lord was not in the earthquake. 12 And after the earthquake there was a fire, but the Lord was not in the fire. And after the fire there was the sound of a gentle whisper. 13 When Elijah heard it, he wrapped his face in his cloak and went out and stood at the entrance of the cave.

And a voice said, "What are you doing here, Elijah?"

14 He replied again, "I have zealously served the Lord God Almighty. But the people of Israel have broken their covenant with you, torn down your altars, and killed every one of your prophets. I am the only one left, and now they are trying to kill me, too."

15 Then the Lord told him, "Go back the same way you came, and travel to the wilderness of Damascus. When you arrive there, anoint Hazael to be king of Aram. 16 Then anoint Jehu grandson of Nimshi to be king of Israel, and anoint Elisha son of Shaphat from the town of Abel-meholah to replace you as my prophet. 17 Anyone who escapes from Hazael will be killed by Jehu, and those who escape Jehu will be killed by Elisha! 18 Yet I will preserve 7,000 others in Israel who have never bowed down to Baal or kissed him!"

Discipleship questions

- **When are you most aware of God's presence and love?**

- **When are you most able to live out of that presence and love?**

- **Under what circumstances are you most likely to seek out his presence?**

- **How does God manifest his love for you?**

- **How might you be able to best grow in experiencing God's presence and love?**

- **What changes might be beneficial to you?**

 Meditation

"There is not in the world a kind of life more sweet and delightful, than that of a continual conversation with God; those only can comprehend it who practice and experience it."

— **Brother Lawrence**

Action step questions

- **In light of our discussion, what is God asking you to do?**

- **How will you obey his prompting?**

- **When will you do it?**

- **Who will help you?**

- **With whom will you share what you have learned before we meet again?**

II. Growing in the knowledge and grace of God

Key question: *In what ways are you seeking to grow in both the knowledge and the grace of God?*

God has placed a hunger within us to know him. We can try many different ways to dampen, ignore, or redirect that hunger, but it remains buried within us. It's part of the natural blueprint of who we are. God made us not only as feeling people but thinking people. We wonder, we question, we evaluate. Our minds hunger to know God and to understand him. Toward that end, we engage with him in much the same way we would engage with another person: we seek to know and understand them. We ask questions, we listen, we observe.

Meditation

"Prayer is not asking. Prayer is putting ... of God, at His disposition, and listening to His voice ..."

Mother Teresa

This week read and reflect daily ... pen a natural flow of conversational prayer with the Holy ... e scriptures, inviting him to reveal himself to you. Then gathe ... longside you and interact over the discipleship questions.

2 Peter 3:18

> Rather, you must grow in ... ur Lord and Savior Jesus Christ.

Psalm 42:1-2

> As the deer longs for ...
> so I long for you, O ...
> 2 I thirst for God, t ...
> When can I go an ...

CONNECT
- What are you thankful for since we met last time?
- Did you share with anyone what you learned last week?
- Did you do what you said you were going to do based upon what you learned last time? What happened as a result?

DISCOVER
- Read through the selected passage twice.
- Retell the passage in your own words.
- What does this passage teach us about God?
- What does this passage teach us about ourselves?

MULTIPLY
- If this is true, what will you do, or how will you live out what you just learned before we meet again?
- What are some struggles or concerns that you, or others, have?
- Is there any way we can meet those needs or concerns as a group?
- Who are you going to tell about what you learned this week?

Colossians 2:1-9

I want you to know how much I have agonized for you and for the church at Laodicea, and for many other believers who have never met me personally. 2 I want them to be encouraged and knit together by strong ties of love. I want them to have complete confidence that they understand God's mysterious plan, which is Christ himself. 3 In him lie hidden all the treasures of wisdom and knowledge.

4 I am telling you this so no one will deceive you with well-crafted arguments. 5 For though I am far away from you, my heart is with you. And I rejoice that you are living as you should and that your faith in Christ is strong.

6 And now, just as you accepted Christ Jesus as your Lord, you must continue to follow him. 7 Let your roots grow down into him, and let your lives be built on him. Then your faith will grow strong in the truth you were taught, and you will overflow with thankfulness.

8 Don't let anyone capture you with empty philosophies and high-sounding nonsense that come from human thinking and from the spiritual powers of this world, rather than from Christ. 9 For in Christ lives all the fullness of God in a human body.

Discipleship questions:

- In what ways are you seeking to know God more deeply?

- What have you learned about God lately?

- How are you growing in knowledge? How are you growing in grace?

- Which qualities of God's character are you deepening your understanding of?

- How do the Father, the Son and the Holy Spirit each help you in your understanding of God?

- How are you experiencing the mystery of God?

- **What effect does the knowledge of God have on your daily life?**

- **In what ways might you continue to grow in this area?**

- **What changes might be beneficial to you?**

Ask God your questions

God is unafraid of our questions and unshaken by our doubts. He is not threatened or diminished in any way by our inquiries. Take some time to write out your questions to God. What do you wonder? What do you want to know? What really matters to you?

 ## *Action steps:*

- **In light of our discussion, what is God asking you to do?**

- **How will you obey his prompting?**

- **When will you do it?**

- **Who will help you?**

- **With whom will you share what you have learned before we meet again?**

III. Reflecting on and applying scripture in your everyday life

Key question: *How are you reflecting on and applying scripture in your everyday life?*

One of the greatest gifts God has given us is his Word, the scriptures. Through the scriptures, we learn more about who God is, what he has done for us, and how we can serve him. All the genres are there: history, poetry, stories, songs, plays, philosophy, apocalyptic literature. It's left to us to figure out how we can best delve into this treasure trove of riches God has given to us.

Different strategies and approaches work best for different people. Some prefer to meditate for a long period of time on a short passage of scripture—reading and rereading it to fully experience the passage. Others prefer to read broad, large portions of scripture to see the overall narrative arc and context of the Word of God. Some don't prefer reading at all, but listening. After all, that's how most people have experienced scripture throughout history: they had it read to them. Memorization is another helpful approach for many in that it allows internalization of the ideas to a greater degree.

One important point is to find out what works for you and do it. As you faithfully interact with scripture, you will meet God there, as the Spirit speaks to you through his Word. The second point is to not walk away from what you are learning, but apply it in your everyday life. Understanding without application is useless.

 Meditation

"I think it would be well, and proper, and obedient, and pure, to grasp your one necessity and not let it go, to dangle from it limp wherever it takes you."
— **Annie Dillard**

This week read and reflect daily on the scripture on the next page. Open a natural flow of conversational prayer with the Holy Spirit as you meditate on the scriptures, inviting him to reveal himself to you. Then gather with those who journey alongside you and interact over the discipleship questions.

2 Timothy 3:16-17

All Scripture is inspired by God and is useful to teach us what is true and to make us realize what is wrong in our lives. It corrects us when we are wrong and teaches us to do what is right. 17 God uses it to prepare and equip his people to do every good work.

Psalm 1:1-3

Oh, the joys of those who do not
  follow the advice of the wicked,
  or stand around with sinners,
  or join in with mockers.
2 But they delight in the law of the Lord,
  meditating on it day and night.
3 They are like trees planted along the riverbank,
  bearing fruit each season.
Their leaves never wither,
  and they prosper in all they do.

Psalm 119:9-16

How can a young person stay pure?
  By obeying your word.
10 I have tried hard to find you—
  don't let me wander from your commands.
11 I have hidden your word in my heart,
  that I might not sin against you.
12 I praise you, O Lord;
  teach me your decrees.
13 I have recited aloud
  all the regulations you have given us.
14 I have rejoiced in your laws
  as much as in riches.
15 I will study your commandments
  and reflect on your ways.
16 I will delight in your decrees
  and not forget your word.

Discipleship questions:

- **How do you best interact with scripture?**

- **What approaches have you tried?**

- **In which ways do you experience two-way communication as you interact with scripture?**

- **Which sections of scripture are you most drawn to and why?**

- **How do you structure your time in scripture? (e.g. a few minutes each day? a larger portion of time once a week?)**

- **Describe a typical time spent interacting with scripture.**

- When is the last time you made a change in your life based on something you learned in scripture? Describe that time.

- When was one time God spoke to you clearly through the scriptures? How did you respond?

- In what ways do you see yourself needing to grow in this area?

- What changes might be beneficial to you?

Conduct a survey

Interview others within the body of Christ about the ways they engage with scripture. Ask them about practices such as mediating on a particular verse, reading large quantities of scripture, memorizing passages, and listening to scripture read aloud. What practices are most meaningful to them? When have they most powerfully experienced God through scripture?

Action steps:

- **In light of our discussion, what is God asking you to do?**

- **How will you obey his prompting?**

- **When will you do it?**

- **Who will help you?**

- **With whom will you share what you have learned before we meet again?**

IV. Dialoguing authentically with God

Key question: *How do you dialogue authentically with God?*

Our experience of God was never intended to be rote: a dutiful prayer asking for things and a routine reading of a chapter of the Bible a day. One of the revolutionary things about Jesus coming to earth incarnate was the communication that this whole worship thing is a relationship. With the death of Jesus, the curtain of the temple was ripped from top to bottom (that's the curtain separating the holy of holies from humanity). That barrier has been broken, and we can enter the presence of God through faith in Jesus, our mediator.

What we have now is not simply a set of duties or a book of rules. It's a real live relationship with another person. What do we do in relationships? We talk. We listen. We laugh. We spend time in each other's presence... sometimes without any agenda at all other than enjoying one another.

Now in the context of a relationship with the creator and Lord of the universe, how does that differ? Certainly, we worship. He is far above us. Yet he is also near, and we had best not remove the relational element. That forms the very core of our worship of God.

Meditation

"The time of business does not differ with me from the time of prayer; and in the noise and clatter of my kitchen, while several persons are at the same time calling for different things, I possess God in as great tranquility as if I were on my knees."

— **Brother Lawrence**

This week read and reflect daily on the scripture on the next page. Open a natural flow of conversational prayer with the Holy Spirit as you meditate on the scriptures, inviting him to reveal himself to you. Then gather with those who journey alongside you and interact over the discipleship questions.

Matthew 27:45-52

At noon, darkness fell across the whole land until three o'clock. 46 At about three o'clock, Jesus called out with a loud voice, "Eli, Eli,lema sabachthani?" which means "My God, my God, why have you abandoned me?"

47 Some of the bystanders misunderstood and thought he was calling for the prophet Elijah. 48 One of them ran and filled a sponge with sour wine, holding it up to him on a reed stick so he could drink. 49 But the rest said, "Wait! Let's see whether Elijah comes to save him."

50 Then Jesus shouted out again, and he released his spirit. 51 At that moment the curtain in the sanctuary of the Temple was torn in two, from top to bottom. The earth shook, rocks split apart, 52 and tombs opened. The bodies of many godly men and women who had died were raised from the dead.

Isaiah 6:1-8

It was in the year King Uzziah died that I saw the Lord. He was sitting on a lofty throne, and the train of his robe filled the Temple. 2 Attending him were mighty seraphim, each having six wings. With two wings they covered their faces, with two they covered their feet, and with two they flew. 3 They were calling out to each other,

"Holy, holy, holy is the Lord of Heaven's Armies!

The whole earth is filled with his glory!"

4 Their voices shook the Temple to its foundations, and the entire building was filled with smoke.

5 Then I said, "It's all over! I am doomed, for I am a sinful man. I have filthy lips, and I live among a people with filthy lips. Yet I have seen the King, the Lord of Heaven's Armies."

6 Then one of the seraphim flew to me with a burning coal he had taken from the altar with a pair of tongs. 7 He touched my lips with it and said, "See, this coal has touched your lips. Now your guilt is removed, and your sins are forgiven."

8 Then I heard the Lord asking, "Whom should I send as a messenger to this people? Who will go for us?"

I said, "Here I am. Send me."

Meditation

"It is impossible to meet God without abandon, without exposing yourself, being raw."

— Bono

Whole life worship

Interview others within the body of Christ about the ways they engage with scripture. Ask them about practices such as mediating on a particular verse, reading large quantities of scripture, memorizing passages, and listening to scripture read aloud. What practices are most meaningful to them? When have they most powerfully experienced God through scripture?

Discipleship questions:

- **What is your understanding of "whole life worship"?**

- **How do you bring your whole self before God?**

- **What else does God want you to bring to the table that you've not yet brought?**

- **In what ways do you feel like you bring your true self before God? In what ways is that hard?**

- **When have you processed your disappointment or anger with God?**

- **When have you experienced awe of God?**

- **In what ways could you further open yourself up to experiencing the presence of God in worship?**

- **What changes might be beneficial to you?**

Action steps:

- **In light of our discussion, what is God asking you to do?**

- **How will you obey his prompting?**

- **When will you do it?**

- **Who will help you?**

- **With whom will you share what you have learned before we meet again?**

V. Worshipping God in spirit and in truth

Key question: *How do you worship God in spirit and in truth as part of your experience of whole life worship?*

We are people designed to worship. If we do not worship God, we will worship something: success, material possessions, another person. How can we worship God in spirit and in truth as he wants to be worshipped?

When people hear the word "worship," they often think of a Sunday morning worship service—something corporate with a large group and singing. That can certainly be part of worship, but worship is much larger than that. In the Old Testament, God set out specific parameters for how we are to approach him in worship and what offerings we are to make to him. Now with the coming of Jesus, a new way of worship has been opened up to us.

It's not a matter of "getting things right" in a religious approach to God, but a matter of approaching God in a manner of "spirit and in truth," in the way Jesus described it to the woman at the well. For each of us that will look different, just as all of creation is varied.

This week read and reflect daily on the scripture on the next page. Open a natural flow of conversational prayer with the Holy Spirit as you meditate on the scriptures, inviting him to reveal himself to you. Then gather with those who journey alongside you and interact over the discipleship questions.

 Meditation

"A man can no more diminish God's glory by refusing to worship Him than a lunatic can put out the sun by scribbling the word 'darkness' on the walls of his cell."

— **C.S. Lewis,** ***The Problem of Pain***

John 4:19-24

"Sir," the woman said, "you must be a prophet. 20 So tell me, why is it that you Jews insist that Jerusalem is the only place of worship, while we Samaritans claim it is here at Mount Gerizim, where our ancestors worshipped?"

21 Jesus replied, "Believe me, dear woman, the time is coming when it will no longer matter whether you worship the Father on this mountain or in Jerusalem. 22 You Samaritans know very little about the one you worship, while we Jews know all about him, for salvation comes through the Jews. 23 But the time is coming—indeed it's here now—when true worshipers will worship the Father in spirit and in truth. The Father is looking for those who will worship him that way. 24 For God is Spirit, so those who worship him must worship in spirit and in truth."

Exodus 33:8-11

Whenever Moses went out to the Tent of Meeting, all the people would get up and stand in the entrances of their own tents. They would all watch Moses until he disappeared inside. 9 As he went into the tent, the pillar of cloud would come down and hover at its entrance while the Lord spoke with Moses. 10 When the people saw the cloud standing at the entrance of the tent, they would stand and bow down in front of their own tents. 11 Inside the Tent of Meeting, the Lord would speak to Moses face to face, as one speaks to a friend. Afterward Moses would return to the camp, but the young man who assisted him, Joshua son of Nun, would remain behind in the Tent of Meeting.

 Meditation

"If all experienced God in the same way and returned Him an identical worship, the song of the Church triumphant would have no symphony, it would be played like an orchestra in which all instruments played the same note."
— **C.S. Lewis**

> ### *Journal:*
>
> What does worshipping in spirit and in truth look like for you? Describe what you look like (where, when, doing what) when you are fully engaged with God in worship.

Discipleship questions:

- **What is your understanding of "worship in spirit and in truth"?**

- **What does that mean for you? What does it not mean?**

- **How do you prepare yourself before coming before God?**

- **How do you see God as you worship him?**

- **What qualities do you sense in God as you worship him?**

- **How do you respond to those qualities?**

- **What changes might be beneficial to you?**

Action steps:

- **In light of our discussion, what is God asking you to do?**

- **How will you obey his prompting?**

- **When will you do it?**

- **Who will help you?**

- **With whom will you share what you have learned before we meet again?**

Guide for Discipling

Spiritual Responsiveness

Listening to the Holy Spirit and acting on what you hear

I. Receiving guidance and empowerment from the Holy Spirit

Key question: *How are you opening yourself up to receive guidance and empowerment from the Holy Spirit?*

We cannot live as we are called to live on our own. We are simply not capable of it. We need the power of the Holy Spirit. Only the Holy Spirit guiding us and speaking to us and empowering us will allow us to respond to what God is calling us to do. We are in a position of need.

How then can we open ourselves to the Holy Spirit? How can we listen for his voice? How can we receive his power? We need to come to God in prayer with a spirit of humility and supplication, recognizing that without the power of the Spirit, we cannot live out what God has called us toward. That power is how the early church was built and how the church continues to be built—through our receiving guidance and empowerment from the Spirit.

When we hear the Spirit calling us to do something, we need to step forward in faith and do it, relying on God to see it through. We can do all things through Christ, who strengths us (Philippians 4:13).

 Meditation

"If God can work through me, he can work through anyone."
— **Saint Francis of Assisi**

Prayer

Ask God to fill you with his power and his Spirit. Ask him to guide you toward what he wants you to do. Ask him to give you a listening ear for his voice and a willing heart to obey it. Then wait in a posture of attentiveness.

This week read and reflect daily on the scripture below. Open a natural flow of conversational prayer with the Holy Spirit as you meditate on the scriptures, inviting him to reveal himself to you. Then gather with those who journey alongside you and interact over the discipleship questions.

Luke 24:49

"And now I will send the Holy Spirit, just as my Father promised. But stay here in the city until the Holy Spirit comes and fills you with power from heaven."

Acts 2:1-21

On the day of Pentecost all the believers were meeting together in one place. 2 Suddenly, there was a sound from heaven like the roaring of a mighty windstorm, and it filled the house where they were sitting. 3 Then, what looked like flames or tongues of fire appeared and settled on each of them. 4 And everyone present was filled with the Holy Spirit and began speaking in other languages, as the Holy Spirit gave them this ability.

5 At that time there were devout Jews from every nation living in Jerusalem. 6 When they heard the loud noise, everyone came running, and they were bewildered to hear their own languages being spoken by the believers.

7 They were completely amazed. "How can this be?" they exclaimed. "These people are all from Galilee, 8 and yet we hear them speaking in our own native languages! 9 Here we are—Parthians, Medes, Elamites, people from Mesopotamia, Judea, Cappadocia, Pontus, the province of Asia, 10 Phrygia, Pamphylia, Egypt, and the areas of Libya around Cyrene, visitors from Rome 11 (both Jews and converts to Judaism), Cretans, and Arabs. And we all hear these people speaking in our own languages about the wonderful things God has done!" 12 They stood there amazed and perplexed. "What can this mean?" they asked each other.

13 But others in the crowd ridiculed them, saying, "They're just drunk, that's all!"

14 Then Peter stepped forward with the eleven other apostles and shouted to the crowd, "Listen carefully, all of you, fellow Jews and residents of Jerusalem! Make no mistake about this. 15 These people are not drunk, as some of you are assuming. Nine o'clock in the morning is much too early for that. 16 No, what you see was predicted long ago by the prophet Joel:

Spiritual Responsiveness

17 *'In the last days,' God says,*
 'I will pour out my Spirit upon all people.
Your sons and daughters will prophesy.
 Your young men will see visions,
 and your old men will dream dreams.
18 *In those days I will pour out my Spirit*
 even on my servants—men and women alike—
 and they will prophesy.
19 *And I will cause wonders in the heavens above*
 and signs on the earth below—
 blood and fire and clouds of smoke.
20 *The sun will become dark,*
 and the moon will turn blood red
 before that great and glorious day of the Lord arrives.
21 *But everyone who calls on the name of the Lord will be saved.'*

Discipleship questions:

- **When are you most aware of relying on the Holy Spirit?**

- **How are you waiting for him?**

- **What are you hearing from the Holy Spirit? How are you listening?**

- **What do you really want God to empower you to do?**

- **How can you pray for one another as you wait to receive guidance and empowerment from the Spirit?**

Action steps:

- **In light of our discussion, what is God asking you to do?**

- **How will you obey his prompting?**

- **When will you do it?**

- **Who will help you?**

- **With whom will you share what you have learned before we meet again?**

II. Discerning opportunities for involvement in God's work

Key question: *Where—and in whom—do you see opportunities to be involved in God's work?*

One of the most powerful recognitions we can have as we respond to the leading of God is that he has already gone before us. We are not alone; he already sent his Holy Spirit to prepare the way. He calls us to be faithful, to do what we can with what we have, but the results of our faithfulness do not lie with us. God is already at work in others long before we come on the scene. He chooses to use us and work through us. Part of our faithfulness is simply paying attention to what God is already doing and following his lead.

 Meditation

"Stop asking God to bless what you're doing. Find out what God's doing. It's already blessed."

— **Bono**

God is at work everywhere—all around us. Look around you. Where can you see him at work? What evidence has he left behind? Where do you sense openness to his Spirit? What questions are people asking?

This week read and reflect daily on the scripture on the next page. Open a natural flow of conversational prayer with the Holy Spirit as you meditate on the scriptures, inviting him to reveal himself to you. Then gather with those who journey alongside you and interact over the discipleship questions.

Luke 19:1-7

Jesus entered Jericho and made his way through the town. 2 There was a man there named Zacchaeus. He was the chief tax collector in the region, and he had become very rich. 3 He tried to get a look at Jesus, but he was too short to see over the crowd.

4 So he ran ahead and climbed a sycamore-fig tree beside the road, for Jesus was going to pass that way.

5 When Jesus came by, he looked up at Zacchaeus and called him by name. "Zacchaeus!" he said. "Quick, come down! I must be a guest in your home today."

6 Zacchaeus quickly climbed down and took Jesus to his house in great excitement and joy. 7 But the people were displeased. "He has gone to be the guest of a notorious sinner," they grumbled.

John 3:1-17

There was a man named Nicodemus, a Jewish religious leader who was a Pharisee. 2 After dark one evening, he came to speak with Jesus. "Rabbi," he said, "we all know that God has sent you to teach us. Your miraculous signs are evidence that God is with you."

3 Jesus replied, "I tell you the truth, unless you are born again, you cannot see the Kingdom of God."

4 "What do you mean?" exclaimed Nicodemus. "How can an old man go back into his mother's womb and be born again?"

5 Jesus replied, "I assure you, no one can enter the Kingdom of God without being born of water and the Spirit. 6 Humans can reproduce only human life, but the Holy Spirit gives birth to spiritual life. 7 So don't be surprised when I say, 'You must be born again.' 8 The wind blows wherever it wants. Just as you can hear the wind but can't tell where it comes from or where it is going, so you can't explain how people are born of the Spirit."

9 "How are these things possible?" Nicodemus asked. 10 Jesus replied, "You are a respected Jewish teacher, and yet you don't understand these things? 11 I assure you, we tell you what we know and have seen, and yet you won't believe our testimony. 12 But if you don't believe me when I tell you about earthly things, how can you possibly believe if I tell you about heavenly things?

13 "No one has ever gone to heaven and returned. But the Son of Man has come down from heaven. 14 And as Moses lifted up the bronze snake on a pole in the wilderness, so the Son of Man must be lifted up, 15 so that everyone who believes in him will have eternal life.

16 "For God loved the world so much that he gave his one and only Son, so that everyone who believes in him will not perish but have eternal life. 17 God sent his Son into the world not to judge the world, but to save the world through him."

Discipleship questions:

- **God is at work everywhere—but where are you currently most sensing his presence and work?**

- **What are some of the different ways God communicates that he's at work somewhere?**

- **What are some of the signs of openness we can see in people?**

- **What are some of the ways we can engage with those who are searching for God?**

- **Where do you sense God working right now?**

Expression through art

Create a painting or drawing that represents to you how you see God at work in the world.

Action steps:

- **In light of our discussion, what is God asking you to do?**

- **How will you obey his prompting?**

- **When will you do it?**

- **Who will help you?**

- **With whom will you share what you have learned before we meet again?**

III. Checking what you're hearing with scripture and your faith community

Key question: *What do you need to check with scripture and your community?*

It's possible we might think we hear God telling us to jump off a bridge. That's why we need to check what we're hearing with scripture and also with our faith community. We don't always hear accurately. If we think we are hearing something that doesn't align with scripture, it's not from God. Don't forget to check what you are hearing against the Word of God, where we know God is speaking.

One thing we also forget on a regular basis is that we need other people. We might remember at breakfast, then forget again by 9:00am. We keep thinking we should be able to do everything on our own, and this stubborn belief certainly extends to what we are hearing from God. When we believe we are hearing something from God, after checking scripture, then the next step is to see if other people are hearing the same thing. Does it line up with what others are hearing? Do others have a perspective on what we're hearing that could be helpful to us? When God is truly at work, he most often orchestrates things so we are not alone in responding to him. We need other people.

 Meditation

"Anyone who doesn't take truth seriously in small matters cannot be trusted in large ones either."

— **Albert Einstein**

This week read and reflect daily on the scriptures on the next page. Open a natural flow of conversational prayer with the Holy Spirit as you meditate on the scriptures, inviting him to reveal himself to you. Then gather with those who journey alongside you and interact over the discipleship questions.

Acts 17:10-12

As soon as it was night, the believers sent Paul and Silas away to Berea. On arriving there, they went to the Jewish synagogue. 11 Now the Berean Jews were of more noble character than those in Thessalonica, for they received the message with great eagerness and examined the Scriptures every day to see if what Paul said was true. 12 Many of them believed, as did also a number of prominent Greek women and many Greek men. (NIV)

Acts 6:1-7

But as the believers rapidly multiplied, there were rumblings of discontent. The Greek-speaking believers complained about the Hebrew-speaking believers, saying that their widows were being discriminated against in the daily distribution of food.

2 So the Twelve called a meeting of all the believers. They said, "We apostles should spend our time teaching the word of God, not running a food program. 3 And so, brothers, select seven men who are well respected and are full of the Spirit and wisdom. We will give them this responsibility. 4 Then we apostles can spend our time in prayer and teaching the word."

5 Everyone liked this idea, and they chose the following: Stephen (a man full of faith and the Holy Spirit), Philip, Procorus, Nicanor, Timon, Parmenas, and Nicolas of Antioch (an earlier convert to the Jewish faith). 6 These seven were presented to the apostles, who prayed for them as they laid their hands on them.

7 So God's message continued to spread. The number of believers greatly increased in Jerusalem, and many of the Jewish priests were converted, too.

Discipleship questions:

- How do you know when you are hearing from God?

- What kinds of "checks" do you perform to see if you are hearing correctly?

- Who do you regularly talk with about what you're hearing from God?

- How do you use scripture to help you make decisions?

- Tell about a time when what you heard from God did not seem to have the backing of your community. How did you navigate that?

Ask three

Ask three people you trust to give you honest, open feedback about what you are hearing from God. Try not to become defensive: just listen. Ask follow up questions as necessary.

Action steps:

- **In light of our discussion, what is God asking you to do?**

- **How will you obey his prompting?**

- **When will you do it?**

- **Who will help you?**

- **With whom will you share what you have learned before we meet again?**

IV. Acting in faith through loving obedience

Key question: *How are you acting in faith through loving obedience?*

The true test of faith is action. Hearing from God matters not at all if we are unwilling to take steps based on what we are hearing. Just as knowledge without putting it to use is void, so is hearing from God and ignoring what he is telling us.

Admittedly, this is easier said than done. There is almost always some element of risk in our obedience, and that risk can range all to the way from martyrdom to looking like a fool. The question is this: What is more important to us... obeying what we are hearing from God or our own self-interests? Our answer to this question is not theoretical; it is borne out in our actions.

This week read and reflect daily on the scripture below. Open a natural flow of conversational prayer with the Holy Spirit as you meditate on the scriptures, inviting him to reveal himself to you. Then gather with those who journey alongside you and interact over the discipleship questions.

 Meditation

> "God doesn't require us to succeed; he only requires that you try."
>
> **— Mother Teresa**

Hebrews 11

> *Faith shows the reality of what we hope for; it is the evidence of things we cannot see. 2 Through their faith, the people in days of old earned a good reputation.*
>
> *3 By faith we understand that the entire universe was formed at God's command, that what we now see did not come from anything that can be seen.*
>
> *4 It was by faith that Abel brought a more acceptable offering to God than Cain did. Abel's offering gave evidence that he was a righteous man, and God showed his approval of his gifts. Although Abel is long dead, he still speaks to us by his example of faith.*

5 It was by faith that Enoch was taken up to heaven without dying—"he disappeared, because God took him." For before he was taken up, he was known as a person who pleased God. 6 And it is impossible to please God without faith. Anyone who wants to come to him must believe that God exists and that he rewards those who sincerely seek him.

7 It was by faith that Noah built a large boat to save his family from the flood. He obeyed God, who warned him about things that had never happened before. By his faith Noah condemned the rest of the world, and he received the righteousness that comes by faith.

8 It was by faith that Abraham obeyed when God called him to leave home and go to another land that God would give him as his inheritance. He went without knowing where he was going. 9 And even when he reached the land God promised him, he lived there by faith—for he was like a foreigner, living in tents. And so did Isaac and Jacob, who inherited the same promise. 10 Abraham was confidently looking forward to a city with eternal foundations, a city designed and built by God.

11 It was by faith that even Sarah was able to have a child, though she was barren and was too old. She believed that God would keep his promise. 12 And so a whole nation came from this one man who was as good as dead—a nation with so many people that, like the stars in the sky and the sand on the seashore, there is no way to count them.

13 All these people died still believing what God had promised them. They did not receive what was promised, but they saw it all from a distance and welcomed it. They agreed that they were foreigners and nomads here on earth. 14 Obviously people who say such things are looking forward to a country they can call their own. 15 If they had longed for the country they came from, they could have gone back. 16 But they were looking for a better place, a heavenly homeland. That is why God is not ashamed to be called their God, for he has prepared a city for them.

17 It was by faith that Abraham offered Isaac as a sacrifice when God was testing him. Abraham, who had received God's promises, was ready to sacrifice his only son, Isaac, 18 even though God had told him, "Isaac is the son through whom your descendants will be counted." 19 Abraham reasoned that if Isaac died, God was able to bring him back to life again. And in a sense, Abraham did receive his son back from the dead.

20 *It was by faith that Isaac promised blessings for the future to his sons, Jacob and Esau.*

21 *It was by faith that Jacob, when he was old and dying, blessed each of Joseph's sons and bowed in worship as he leaned on his staff.*

22 *It was by faith that Joseph, when he was about to die, said confidently that the people of Israel would leave Egypt. He even commanded them to take his bones with them when they left.*

23 *It was by faith that Moses' parents hid him for three months when he was born. They saw that God had given them an unusual child, and they were not afraid to disobey the king's command.*

24 *It was by faith that Moses, when he grew up, refused to be called the son of Pharaoh's daughter. 25 He chose to share the oppression of God's people instead of enjoying the fleeting pleasures of sin. 26 He thought it was better to suffer for the sake of Christ than to own the treasures of Egypt, for he was looking ahead to his great reward. 27 It was by faith that Moses left the land of Egypt, not fearing the king's anger. He kept right on going because he kept his eyes on the one who is invisible. 28 It was by faith that Moses commanded the people of Israel to keep the Passover and to sprinkle blood on the doorposts so that the angel of death would not kill their firstborn sons.*

29 *It was by faith that the people of Israel went right through the Red Sea as though they were on dry ground. But when the Egyptians tried to follow, they were all drowned.*

30 *It was by faith that the people of Israel marched around Jericho for seven days, and the walls came crashing down.*

31 *It was by faith that Rahab the prostitute was not destroyed with the people in her city who refused to obey God. For she had given a friendly welcome to the spies.*

32 *How much more do I need to say? It would take too long to recount the stories of the faith of Gideon, Barak, Samson, Jephthah, David, Samuel, and all the prophets. 33 By faith these people overthrew kingdoms, ruled with justice, and received what God had promised them. They shut the mouths of lions, 34 quenched the flames of fire, and escaped death by the edge of the sword. Their weakness was turned to strength. They became strong in battle and put whole armies to flight.*

35 Women received their loved ones back again from death.

But others were tortured, refusing to turn from God in order to be set free. They placed their hope in a better life after the resurrection. 36 Some were jeered at, and their backs were cut open with whips. Others were chained in prisons. 37 Some died by stoning, some were sawed in half, and others were killed with the sword. Some went about wearing skins of sheep and goats, destitute and oppressed and mistreated.

38 They were too good for this world, wandering over deserts and mountains, hiding in caves and holes in the ground.

39 All these people earned a good reputation because of their faith, yet none of them received all that God had promised. 40 For God had something better in mind for us, so that they would not reach perfection without us.

Discipleship questions:

- Tell about a time when you felt God was asking you to do something that made you afraid. What happened?

- How do you see the difference between faith and certainty?

- What are some steps of faith that you have seen God call you or others to take?

- When is obedience hardest for you? When is obedience easiest?

- What actions do you feel God might be calling you toward? How do you feel about that?

Action steps:

- **In light of our discussion, what is God asking you to do?**

- **How will you obey his prompting?**

- **When will you do it?**

- **Who will help you?**

- **With whom will you share what you have learned before we meet again?**

V. Listening for God's calling in your life

Key question: *How are you listening for God's calling for your life?*

The term "calling" has been interpreted many different ways. Many believers have spent years disengaged from ministry while waiting for a supernatural communication from God. Sometimes God gives those types of miraculous signs: the apostle Paul was practically struck by lightning and told what to do with the rest of his life. However, that's not the case for most of us. Yet that doesn't mean we don't have a calling; it just means we have a different way of finding that calling.

God has something for every believer to do in this life. We all have a contribution to make toward the coming of his Kingdom. Our task is to listen to God's voice, to live in obedience to the commands God has given all people, and to discern as we go what else God would have us do. But even when we don't have a clear direction, we are still to be in motion. The basic principles of motion are that an object in motion tends to stay in motion, and an object at rest tends to stay at rest.

As we move forward in obedience to what we already know to do, more direction will be given to us by the Holy Spirit.

This week read and reflect daily on the scripture on the next page. Open a natural flow of conversational prayer with the Holy Spirit as you meditate on the scriptures, inviting him to reveal himself to you. Then gather with those who journey alongside you and interact over the discipleship questions.

 Meditation

"An object in motion tends to remain in motion, and an object at rest tends to remain at rest."

— **Isaac Newton, first law of motions**

Matthew 4:18-20

One day as Jesus was walking along the shore of the Sea of Galilee, he saw two brothers—Simon, also called Peter, and Andrew—throwing a net into the water, for they fished for a living. 19 Jesus called out to them, "Come, follow me, and I will show you how to fish for people!" 20 And they left their nets at once and followed him.

Mark 5:18-20

As Jesus was getting into the boat, the man who had been demon possessed begged to go with him. 19 But Jesus said, "No, go home to your family, and tell them everything the Lord has done for you and how merciful he has been." 20 So the man started off to visit the Ten Towns of that region and began to proclaim the great things Jesus had done for him; and everyone was amazed at what he told them.

Ephesians 4:1-6

Therefore I, a prisoner for serving the Lord, beg you to lead a life worthy of your calling, for you have been called by God. 2 Always be humble and gentle. Be patient with each other, making allowance for each other's faults because of your love. 3 Make every effort to keep yourselves united in the Spirit, binding yourselves together with peace. 4 For there is one body and one Spirit, just as you have been called to one glorious hope for the future. 5 There is one Lord, one faith, one baptism, 6 and one God and Father, who is over all and in all and living through all.

Philippians 3:12-14

I don't mean to say that I have already achieved these things or that I have already reached perfection. But I press on to possess that perfection for which Christ Jesus first possessed me. 13 No, dear brothers and sisters, I have not achieved it, but I focus on this one thing: Forgetting the past and looking forward to what lies ahead, 14 I press on to reach the end of the race and receive the heavenly prize for which God, through Christ Jesus, is calling us.

1 Timothy 6:12

Fight the good fight for the true faith. Hold tightly to the eternal life to which God has called you, which you have confessed so well before many witnesses.

 **Meditation**

"A dead thing goes with the stream, but only a living thing can go against it."

— **G.K. Chesterton,** *The Everlasting Man*

Discipleship questions:

- **How do you understand God's call for your life?**

- **What are some of the things he calls all believers to?**

- **How will you discern those things he is calling you specifically to?**

- **What practices can help you seek out God's calling in your life?**

- **How do God's calling and your desires fit together?**

Exercise

What do you already know God wants you to do? Search the scriptures for commands. Write down as many as you can.

Action steps:

- **In light of our discussion, what is God asking you to do?**

- **How will you obey his prompting?**

- **When will you do it?**

- **Who will help you?**

- **With whom will you share what you have learned before we meet again?**

Sacrificial Service

Doing good works even when it's costly,
inconvenient or challenging

I. Blessing others with your words and deeds

Key questions: *How are you blessing others with your words? How are you blessing others with your deeds?*

A cup of cold water can speak volumes. A generous word can be like water on parched land. We don't know how much we need it until someone takes the time to give it to us. Consider the acts of service we can do for one another: caring for someone else's child, offering your skills when they are needed, giving someone a ride to the airport. These are small things that make a difference because of the messages they send.

We love with not only actions, but with words. Consider the messages we have the power to give one another: You are loved. You have value. Your contribution matters. These are words of life that have the potential to make deep, long-term impact. The things we have learned and received, we have the power to pass on to others. In yet another miracle, even the things we have not received ourselves we have the power to pass on to others. We may not have been loved well as a child, but we have the power to love a child well because of the great love God has poured out on us. Sacrificial serving opens a wellspring of abundance in this way, giving life not only to ourselves, but to others.

Meditation

"Similarly, the impulse to keep to yourself what you have learned is not only shameful, it is destructive. Anything you do not give freely and abundantly becomes lost to you. You open your safe and find ashes."

— **Annie Dillard, *The Writing Life***

This week read and reflect on the scripture below. Open a natural flow of conversational prayer with the Holy Spirit as you meditate on the scriptures, inviting him to reveal himself to you. Then gather with those who journey alongside you and interact over the discipleship questions.

John 15:12-14

My command is this: Love each other as I have loved you. 13 Greater love has no one than this: to lay down one's life for one's friends. 14 You are my friends if you do what I command. (NIV)

Luke 10:25-37

One day an expert in religious law stood up to test Jesus by asking him this question: "Teacher, what should I do to inherit eternal life?"

26 Jesus replied, "What does the law of Moses say? How do you read it?"

27 The man answered, "'You must love the Lord your God with all your heart, all your soul, all your strength, and all your mind.' And, 'Love your neighbor as yourself.'"

28 "Right!" Jesus told him. "Do this and you will live!"

29 The man wanted to justify his actions, so he asked Jesus, "And who is my neighbor?"

30 Jesus replied with a story: "A Jewish man was traveling from Jerusalem down to Jericho, and he was attacked by bandits. They stripped him of his clothes, beat him up, and left him half dead beside the road.

31 "By chance a priest came along. But when he saw the man lying there, he crossed to the other side of the road and passed him by. 32 A Temple assistant walked over and looked at him lying there, but he also passed by on the other side.

33 "Then a despised Samaritan came along, and when he saw the man, he felt compassion for him. 34 Going over to him, the Samaritan soothed his wounds with olive oil and wine and bandaged them. Then he put the man on his own donkey and took him to an inn, where he took care of him. 35 The next day he handed the innkeeper two silver coins, telling him, 'Take care of this man. If his bill runs higher than this, I'll pay you the next time I'm here.'

36 "Now which of these three would you say was a neighbor to the man who was attacked by bandits?" Jesus asked.

37 The man replied, "The one who showed him mercy."

Then Jesus said, "Yes, now go and do the same."

 Meditation

"A life not lived for others is not a life."

— **Mother Teresa**

Discipleship questions:

- **How are you blessing others with your words?**

- **How are you blessing others with your deeds?**

- **Who do you know who needs blessing?**

- **What are your impressions of the story of the good Samaritan?**

Telling the story

Tell the story of the good Samaritan from the following perspectives:
- The traveling man
- The priest
- The Samaritan
- The innkeeper

Action steps:

- **In light of our discussion, what is God asking you to do?**

- **How will you obey his prompting?**

- **When will you do it?**

- **Who will help you?**

- **With whom will you share what you have learned before we meet again?**

II. Partnering with others to minister in practical ways

Key question: *How are you partnering with others to minister in practical ways?*

Good news that is really good news has practical implications. It matters to people. It makes a difference in their everyday lives. If your ministry is not doing that, how are you reflecting Jesus to people? When Jesus was asked for proof that he was the Messiah, he cited the practical implications of his ministry. Our ministry, though likely less miraculous, should reflect the presence of Jesus in practical ways as well.

We are going to need others alongside us to do this. Very little that makes a big difference can be done by one person alone. Consider who you can partner with to serve others. Each person will have a unique contribution to make to the whole. Look around you to the needs of the community. What would show the presence of God to these particular people? What would be good news to them?

This week read and reflect daily on the scripture below. Open a natural flow of conversational prayer with the Holy Spirit as you meditate on the scriptures, inviting him to reveal himself to you. Then gather with those who journey alongside you and interact over the discipleship questions.

Matthew 11:2-6

> *John the Baptist, who was in prison, heard about all the things the Messiah was doing. So he sent his disciples to ask Jesus, 3 "Are you the Messiah we've been expecting, or should we keep looking for someone else?"*
>
> *4 Jesus told them, "Go back to John and tell him what you have heard and seen— 5 the blind see, the lame walk, the lepers are cured, the deaf hear, the dead are raised to life, and the Good News is being preached to the poor. 6 And tell him, 'God blesses those who do not turn away because of me.'"*

Titus 3:14

> *Our people must learn to do good by meeting the urgent needs of others; then they will not be unproductive.*

James 1:27

> *Pure and genuine religion in the sight of God the Father means caring for orphans and widows in their distress and refusing to let the world corrupt you.*

Needs List

Make a list of the needs in your community. Think big, think small. List as many as you can. What would feel like good news to these people? Put each one on a post-it note. Then gather with others and pick one post-it note each that you feel God is calling you to address.

Discipleship questions:

- **Who is working alongside you to minister to others?**

- **What are some unique gifts and contributions they offer?**

- **Who do you sense God calling you to minister to?**

- **What needs do you see around you?**

- **Which of the needs in your community are you able to address?**

- **How might you best do that?**

Action steps:

- In light of our discussion, what is God asking you to do?

- How will you obey his prompting?

- When will you do it?

- Who will help you?

- With whom will you share what you have learned before we meet again?

III. Ministering personally and appropriately to the poor

Key question: *How are you ministering personally and appropriately to the poor?*

As followers of Jesus, we are called to serve all people. Yet there is something uniquely selfless about serving the poor and the oppressed and the helpless. These are the people who cannot pay us back. They are the same people to whom Jesus opened the doors of the Kingdom wide. God calls the poor, the weary, and the downtrodden to himself to give them rest... and he expects to use us as his hands to do that work. We are the hands and feet of Jesus to a world that cannot help itself. Indeed, acts of service to the poor are one of the only cases in scripture where God promises rewards and blessings.

We are called to serve the poor in a personal way. That means more than just sending a check. As we interact with the poor, God wants to do work in us as well. We can engage with them as unique individuals made in the image of God, equals to ourselves and our friends and our family. We are to treat them with respect and serve them in ways that will benefit their everyday lives and their growth.

This week read and reflect daily on the scripture below. Open a natural flow of conversational prayer with the Holy Spirit as you meditate on the scriptures, inviting him to reveal himself to you. Then gather with those who journey alongside you and interact over the discipleship questions.

Matthew 22:1-10

> *Jesus also told them other parables. He said, 2 "The Kingdom of Heaven can be illustrated by the story of a king who prepared a great wedding feast for his son. 3 When the banquet was ready, he sent his servants to notify those who were invited. But they all refused to come!*
>
> *4 "So he sent other servants to tell them, 'The feast has been prepared. The bulls and fattened cattle have been killed, and everything is ready. Come to the banquet!' 5 But the guests he had invited ignored them and went their own way, one to his farm, another to his business. 6 Others seized his messengers and insulted them and killed them.*
>
> *7 "The king was furious, and he sent out his army to destroy the murderers and burn their town.*

8 "And he said to his servants, 'The wedding feast is ready, and the guests I invited aren't worthy of the honor. 9 Now go out to the street corners and invite everyone you see.' 10 So the servants brought in everyone they could find, good and bad alike, and the banquet hall was filled with guests."

Galatians 2:10

Their only suggestion was that we keep on helping the poor, which I have always been eager to do.

Matthew 5:46-47

If you love only those who love you, what reward is there for that? Even corrupt tax collectors do that much. 47 If you are kind only to your friends, how are you different from anyone else? Even pagans do that.

Matthew 25:31-46

"But when the Son of Man comes in his glory, and all the angels with him, then he will sit upon his glorious throne. 32 All the nations will be gathered in his presence, and he will separate the people as a shepherd separates the sheep from the goats. 33 He will place the sheep at his right hand and the goats at his left.

34 "Then the King will say to those on his right, 'Come, you who are blessed by my Father, inherit the Kingdom prepared for you from the creation of the world. 35 For I was hungry, and you fed me. I was thirsty, and you gave me a drink. I was a stranger, and you invited me into your home. 36 I was naked, and you gave me clothing. I was sick, and you cared for me. I was in prison, and you visited me.'

37 "Then these righteous ones will reply, 'Lord, when did we ever see you hungry and feed you? Or thirsty and give you something to drink? 38 Or a stranger and show you hospitality? Or naked and give you clothing? 39 When did we ever see you sick or in prison and visit you?'

40 "And the King will say, 'I tell you the truth, when you did it to one of the least of these my brothers and sisters, you were doing it to me!'

41 "Then the King will turn to those on the left and say, 'Away with you, you cursed ones, into the eternal fire prepared for the devil and his demons. 42 For I was hungry, and you didn't feed me. I was thirsty, and you didn't give me a drink.

43 I was a stranger, and you didn't invite me into your home. I was naked, and you didn't give me clothing. I was sick and in prison, and you didn't visit me.'

44 "Then they will reply, 'Lord, when did we ever see you hungry or thirsty or a stranger or naked or sick or in prison, and not help you?'

45 "And he will answer, 'I tell you the truth, when you refused to help the least of these my brothers and sisters, you were refusing to help me.'

46 "And they will go away into eternal punishment, but the righteous will go into eternal life."

 ## *Meditation*

"At the end of life we will not be judged by how many diplomas we have received, how much money we have made, how many great things we have done. We will be judged by 'I was hungry, and you gave me something to eat, I was naked and you clothed me. I was homeless, and you took me in.'"

— Mother Teresa

Discipleship questions:

- **Who are the poor?**

- **What do they need?**

- **How are you ministering personally?**

- **How are you ministering appropriately?**

- **In what ways is your ministry proactive and in what ways is it reactive?**

- **How are you contributing to long-term change?**

☛ **How are you changing because of your involvement with the poor?**

Throw a party

Start planning a party like the one described in Matthew 22... a party with the doors thrown wide open. Who might you invite?

Action steps:

- **In light of our discussion, what is God asking you to do?**

- **How will you obey his prompting?**

- **When will you do it?**

- **Who will help you?**

- **With whom will you share what you have learned before we meet again?**

IV. Speaking up for people experiencing injustice

Key question: *How are you speaking up for people experiencing injustice?*

None of us have to look far to find injustices in the world. Some injustices are more obvious than others. Some injustices we are less sensitive to than others. But wherever we are in this fallen world that is not as it was intended to be, we can see injustice around us. The question is, as followers of Jesus, what will we do about it? Will we be silent, saying that's just the way it is? Or will we risk speaking out? For there is often a cost.

 Meditation

"Silence in the face of evil is itself evil: God will not hold us guiltless. Not to speak is to speak. Not to act is to act."

— **Dietrich Bonhoeffer**

Consider the time of slavery in the United States. Followers of Jesus who spoke out against these practices were maligned and marginalized, even by other groups that called themselves Christians. Yet they spoke out and did what was right, fighting injustice. Two hundred years from now, when people look back on our time, what injustices will they be looking to see if we took on? What broken systems and unjust practices are we taking steps to change? Whether we are successful or not is a secondary issue. The primary issue is whether we are willing to try at all.

Injustice isn't just about broad social issues. It's personal. It has a face. Consider specific people who are currently experiencing injustice. How can you speak out for them?

 Meditation

"We are not to simply bandage the wounds of victims beneath the wheels of injustice, we are to drive a spoke into the wheel itself."

— **Dietrich Bonhoeffer**

This week read and reflect daily on the scripture below. Open a natural flow of conversational prayer with the Holy Spirit as you meditate on the scriptures, inviting him to reveal himself to you. Then gather with those who journey alongside you and interact over the discipleship questions.

Amos 5:7-24

> You twist justice, making it a bitter pill for the oppressed.
>   You treat the righteous like dirt.
>
> 8 It is the Lord who created the stars,
>   the Pleiades and Orion.
> He turns darkness into morning
>   and day into night.
> He draws up water from the oceans
>   and pours it down as rain on the land.
>   The Lord is his name!
> 9 With blinding speed and power he destroys the strong,
>   crushing all their defenses.
>
> 10 How you hate honest judges!
>   How you despise people who tell the truth!
> 11 You trample the poor,
>   stealing their grain through taxes and unfair rent.
> Therefore, though you build beautiful stone houses,
>   you will never live in them.
> Though you plant lush vineyards,
>   you will never drink wine from them.
> 12 For I know the vast number of your sins
>   and the depth of your rebellions.
> You oppress good people by taking bribes
>   and deprive the poor of justice in the courts.
> 13 So those who are smart keep their mouths shut,
>   for it is an evil time.
>
> 14 Do what is good and run from evil
>   so that you may live!
> Then the Lord God of Heaven's Armies will be your helper,
>   just as you have claimed.

15 *Hate evil and love what is good;*
   turn your courts into true halls of justice.
Perhaps even yet the Lord God of Heaven's Armies
   will have mercy on the remnant of his people.

16 *Therefore, this is what the Lord, the Lord God of Heaven's Armies, says:*

"There will be crying in all the public squares
   and mourning in every street.
Call for the farmers to weep with you,
   and summon professional mourners to wail.
17 *There will be wailing in every vineyard,*
   for I will destroy them all,"
   says the Lord.

18 *What sorrow awaits you who say,*
   "If only the day of the Lord were here!"
You have no idea what you are wishing for.
   That day will bring darkness, not light.
19 *In that day you will be like a man who runs from a lion — only to meet a bear.*
   Escaping from the bear, he leans his hand against a wall in his house — and he's bitten by a snake.
20 *Yes, the day of the Lord will be dark and hopeless,*
   without a ray of joy or hope.

21 *"I hate all your show and pretense—*
   the hypocrisy of your religious festivals and solemn assemblies.
22 *I will not accept your burnt offerings and grain offerings.*
   I won't even notice all your choice peace offerings.
23 *Away with your noisy hymns of praise!*
   I will not listen to the music of your harps.
24 *Instead, I want to see a mighty flood of justice,*
   an endless river of righteous living.

Discipleship questions:

- **Who do you know who is currently experiencing injustice?**

- **What are you doing in that situation?**

- **What injustices do you feel most keenly?**

- **What can you do about them?**

- **What risk might that involve for you personally?**

- **What rewards might there be?**

- **What historical figures do you most admire for the ways in which they stood in the way of injustice? How could you emulate them?**

Conduct a survey:

Everyone cares about something. God places different burdens on different people's hearts... and that extends to people who don't yet know him. Interview some people within your community to find out what injustices they feel most keenly. What just feels wrong to them in their bones?

Action steps:

- **In light of our discussion, what is God asking you to do?**

- **How will you obey his prompting?**

- **When will you do it?**

- **Who will help you?**

- **With whom will you share what you have learned before we meet again?**

V. Cultivating a compassionate heart

Key question: *How are you cultivating a compassionate heart within yourself?*

We are to be people who care, and out of that care, pray that God will bring about his needed work. Yet cultivating compassion is harder to do than simply taking certain actions or steps. To cultivate compassion, we need to open ourselves up to the pain and the needs of others. That is inherently frightening, threatening to overwhelm us without divine help. Imagine standing in the midst of a sea of beggars asking for food, and you only have so much to give. Our natural inclination is to run, to find a way to protect ourselves. For caring—at a deep and authentic level of our spirits—opens us up to pain.

Compassion not only makes us vulnerable to pain, but it puts us face to face with our own sense of inadequacy. We know we are not strong enough, rich enough, smart enough to solve people's problems. We are not God; we can only do so much. That's why we bring these needs before him in prayer. We alone cannot bring healing and reconciliation, but we can experience the power of God working through us as we rely on him and listen to his voice and direction.

Meditation

"To love at all is to be vulnerable. Love anything and your heart will be wrung and possibly broken. If you want to make sure of keeping it intact you must give it to no one, not even an animal. Wrap it carefully round with hobbies and little luxuries; avoid all entanglements. Lock it up safe in the casket or coffin of your selfishness. But in that casket, safe, dark, motionless, airless, it will change. It will not be broken; it will become unbreakable, impenetrable, irredeemable. To love is to be vulnerable."

— **C.S. Lewis**

This week read and reflect daily on the scripture below. Open a natural flow of conversational prayer with the Holy Spirit as you meditate on the scriptures, inviting him to reveal himself to you. Then gather with those who journey alongside you and interact over the discipleship questions.

Matthew 9:36-38

When he saw the crowds, he had compassion on them because they were confused and helpless, like sheep without a shepherd. 37 He said to his disciples, "The harvest is great, but the workers are few. 38 So pray to the Lord who is in charge of the harvest; ask him to send more workers into his fields."

Matthew 14:14

Jesus saw the huge crowd as he stepped from the boat, and he had compassion on them and healed their sick.

Matthew 15:32

Jesus called his disciples to him and said, "I have compassion for these people; they have already been with me three days and have nothing to eat. I do not want to send them away hungry, or they may collapse on the way." (NIV)

Matthew 20:34

Jesus had compassion on them and touched their eyes. Immediately they received their sight and followed him. (NIV)

1 Peter 3:8-9

Finally, all of you, be like-minded, be sympathetic, love one another, be compassionate and humble. 9 Do not repay evil with evil or insult with insult. On the contrary, repay evil with blessing, because to this you were called so that you may inherit a blessing. (NIV)

Prayer

Ask God to show you who he is sending you to. We all live as sent people—who specifically are you sent to? Who do you feel compassion for? Whose plight or difficulties upset you? Ask God to break your heart over the things that break his heart. Ask him for healing and reconciliation.

Discipleship questions:

- How would you describe the role of compassion in your life?

- For whom do you feel compassion? How do you demonstrate that compassion?

- What evidence of compassion do you see in the life of Jesus? Through what actions did he demonstrate it?

- What practices might help you grow in compassion?

- How have you seen God work in your life because of a step or risk you took in serving others?

Action steps:

- **In light of our discussion, what is God asking you to do?**

- **How will you obey his prompting?**

- **When will you do it?**

- **Who will help you?**

- **With whom will you share what you have learned before we meet again?**

 Meditation

"At a certain point, I just felt, you know, God is not looking for alms, God is looking for action."

— **Bono**

Generous Living

Faithfully stewarding what God has given you
for the advancement of the Kingdom

I. Managing your time and resources for kingdom purposes

Key question: *How are you managing your time and resources for kingdom purposes?*

God has entrusted certain resources to each of us: resources we are to use for his Kingdom. We are to steward them wisely in a holistic sense: saving, investing, giving. Having a good overall stewardship strategy in our lives puts us in a better position to live generously in all the myriad ways God would have us be generous.

Meditation

"Abundance isn't God's provision for me to live in luxury. It's his provision for me to help others live. God entrusts me with his money not to build my kingdom on earth, but to build his kingdom in heaven."

— **Randy Alcorn**

Too often we think only of money when we think of generosity. But what else has God entrusted to us? If we have an abundance of time due to being unemployed or retired, we can use that for prayer and service. If we have a home, we can use that to welcome others. If we speak English, we can teach the language to international students. If we can read, we can tutor children. If we are well-connected socially, we can connect people with one another who can band then together for Kingdom purposes. There are many, many ways God has gifted us that we seldom recognize.

Make an accounting of your assets

Write down a list of all that God has entrusted to you: time, gifts, resources, situations, abilities, etc. List as many as you can. Now pray over each of these assets and ask God how he would have you steward it for his kingdom.

This week read and reflect daily on the scripture below. Open a natural flow of conversational prayer with the Holy Spirit as you meditate on the scriptures, inviting him to reveal himself to you. Then gather with those who journey alongside you and interact over the discipleship questions.

Matthew 25:14-30

"Again, the Kingdom of Heaven can be illustrated by the story of a man going on a long trip. He called together his servants and entrusted his money to them while he was gone. 15 He gave five bags of silver to one, two bags of silver to another, and one bag of silver to the last—dividing it in proportion to their abilities. He then left on his trip.

16 "The servant who received the five bags of silver began to invest the money and earned five more. 17 The servant with two bags of silver also went to work and earned two more. 18 But the servant who received the one bag of silver dug a hole in the ground and hid the master's money.

19 "After a long time their master returned from his trip and called them to give an account of how they had used his money. 20 The servant to whom he had entrusted the five bags of silver came forward with five more and said, 'Master, you gave me five bags of silver to invest, and I have earned five more.'

21 "The master was full of praise. 'Well done, my good and faithful servant. You have been faithful in handling this small amount, so now I will give you many more responsibilities. Let's celebrate together!'

22 "The servant who had received the two bags of silver came forward and said, 'Master, you gave me two bags of silver to invest, and I have earned two more.'

23 "The master said, 'Well done, my good and faithful servant. You have been faithful in handling this small amount, so now I will give you many more responsibilities. Let's celebrate together!'

24 "Then the servant with the one bag of silver came and said, 'Master, I knew you were a harsh man, harvesting crops you didn't plant and gathering crops you didn't cultivate. 25 I was afraid I would lose your money, so I hid it in the earth. Look, here is your money back.'

26 "But the master replied, 'You wicked and lazy servant! If you knew I harvested crops I didn't plant and gathered crops I didn't cultivate,

27 why didn't you deposit my money in the bank? At least I could have gotten some interest on it.'

28 "Then he ordered, 'Take the money from this servant, and give it to the one with the ten bags of silver. 29 To those who use well what they are given, even more will be given, and they will have an abundance. But from those who do nothing, even what little they have will be taken away. 30 Now throw this useless servant into outer darkness, where there will be weeping and gnashing of teeth.'"

Discipleship questions:

- What have you become aware of God gifting you with?

- What opportunities do you have for using those gifts?

- What would it look like to bury it in the ground? What would it look like to invest it?

- What is the risk you would need to take to invest what God has entrusted you with?

Action steps:

- **In light of our discussion, what is God asking you to do?**

- **How will you obey his prompting?**

- **When will you do it?**

- **Who will help you?**

- **With whom will you share what you have learned before we meet again?**

II. Using your spiritual gifts to bless others

Key question: *How are you using your gifts to bless others?*

We all have different gifts—that's the point of the Body of Christ. Each of us is incomplete without the rest. Individually, we each make a difference in only a small way. Collectively, the impact is huge. Consider your gifts. What are you good at? What do other people say you are good at? How has God used you in the past? What are you passionate about doing? How can you do that for the glory of God?

Meditation

"If you think you are too small to make a difference, try sleeping with a mosquito."

— **Dalai Lama XIV**

Spiritual gifts are an important place to start when we consider serving others, but we need to remember that God can use us outside of our giftedness too. Sometimes God places us in situations outside of our comfort zones or has us working in areas where we feel out of our depths. Those can be significant growing experiences for us. Looked at from a practical standpoint, Jesus' primary gift was probably not washing feet... but he did it anyway. Likewise, we are to have a servant's heart as we go about serving others. No task is too small or too unimportant.

Whole life worship

Take a look at the list of spiritual gifts below. Although these were all drawn from scripture, the list may be incomplete. Next to each gift, write the name of at least one person you believe is gifted in that way. When you've finished, look down the list and spend some time praying and envisioning what God might have you do.

Prophecy _____

Serving _____

Teaching _____

Exhortation _____

Giving _____

Leadership _____

Discernment _____

Hospitality _____

Healing _____

Apostleship _____

Evangelism _____

Mercy _____

Faith _____

Administration _____

Shepherding _____

This week read and reflect daily on the scripture on the next page. Open a natural flow of conversational prayer with the Holy Spirit as you meditate on the scriptures, inviting him to reveal himself to you. Then gather with those who journey alongside you and interact over the discipleship questions.

Romans 12:3-21

Because of the privilege and authority God has given me, I give each of you this warning: Don't think you are better than you really are. Be honest in your evaluation of yourselves, measuring yourselves by the faith God has given us. 4 Just as our bodies have many parts and each part has a special function, 5 so it is with Christ's body. We are many parts of one body, and we all belong to each other.

6 In his grace, God has given us different gifts for doing certain things well. So if God has given you the ability to prophesy, speak out with as much faith as God has given you. 7 If your gift is serving others, serve them well. If you are a teacher, teach well. 8 If your gift is to encourage others, be encouraging. If it is giving, give generously. If God has given you leadership ability, take the responsibility seriously. And if you have a gift for showing kindness to others, do it gladly.

9 Don't just pretend to love others. Really love them. Hate what is wrong. Hold tightly to what is good. 10 Love each other with genuine affection, and take delight in honoring each other. 11 Never be lazy, but work hard and serve the Lord enthusiastically. 12 Rejoice in our confident hope. Be patient in trouble, and keep on praying. 13 When God's people are in need, be ready to help them. Always be eager to practice hospitality.

14 Bless those who persecute you. Don't curse them; pray that God will bless them. 15 Be happy with those who are happy, and weep with those who weep. 16 Live in harmony with each other. Don't be too proud to enjoy the company of ordinary people. And don't think you know it all!

17 Never pay back evil with more evil. Do things in such a way that everyone can see you are honorable. 18 Do all that you can to live in peace with everyone.

19 Dear friends, never take revenge. Leave that to the righteous anger of God. For the Scriptures say,

"I will take revenge;
* I will pay them back,"*
* says the Lord.*

20 Instead,
"If your enemies are hungry, feed them.
* If they are thirsty, give them something to drink.*
In doing this, you will heap
* burning coals of shame on their heads."*

21 Don't let evil conquer you, but conquer evil by doing good.

Discipleship questions:

- **What gifts has God specifically given you?**

- **For what purpose do you believe he has given them to you?**

- **How could you best use those gifts in your current environment?**

- **What are some unique contributions you can make?**

- **What are some creative ways you might use your gifts in the future?**

- **What might result?**

Action steps:

- **In light of our discussion, what is God asking you to do?**

- **How will you obey his prompting?**

- **When will you do it?**

- **Who will help you?**

- **With whom will you share what you have learned before we meet again?**

III. Giving your money generously and wisely

Key question: *How are you giving your money and resources?*

Just as our time and our spiritual gifts are not to be used for ourselves alone, so our money, our property, and our resources are not to be used for ourselves alone. These things are gifts God has blessed us with, and he means for us to use them to bless others in turn. We are to practice generosity in all areas of our lives. That includes our finances. Money can be a hard thing for people to talk about. In most cultures, people are very private about financial matters. Yet God expects to be let into the most private areas of our lives. He tells us not to cling to our possessions for identity but to cling to him.

As we give, we need to be generous. We need to offer our money with open hands, recognizing that it is not really our money, but God's. We are stewards. At the same time—because we are stewards—we are to give wisely. We are to give in ways that forward the work of the kingdom, that bring redemption and hope to the poor, and that help others come into a position where they will be able to give generously and wisely as well.

 Meditation

"Give a bowl of rice to a man and you will feed him for a day. Teach him how to grow his own rice and you will save his life."

— **Confucius**

This week read and reflect daily on the scripture on the next page. Open a natural flow of conversational prayer with the Holy Spirit as you meditate on the scriptures, inviting him to reveal himself to you. Then gather with those who journey alongside you and interact over the discipleship questions.

Luke 12:15-21

Then he said, "Beware! Guard against every kind of greed. Life is not measured by how much you own."

16 Then he told them a story: "A rich man had a fertile farm that produced fine crops. 17 He said to himself, 'What should I do? I don't have room for all my crops.'

18 Then he said, 'I know! I'll tear down my barns and build bigger ones. Then I'll have room enough to store all my wheat and other goods. 19 And I'll sit back and say to myself, "My friend, you have enough stored away for years to come. Now take it easy! Eat, drink, and be merry!"'

20 "But God said to him, 'You fool! You will die this very night. Then who will get everything you worked for?'

21 "Yes, a person is a fool to store up earthly wealth but not have a rich relationship with God."

Matthew 6:1-4, 19-21

"Watch out! Don't do your good deeds publicly, to be admired by others, for you will lose the reward from your Father in heaven. 2 When you give to someone in need, don't do as the hypocrites do—blowing trumpets in the synagogues and streets to call attention to their acts of charity! I tell you the truth, they have received all the reward they will ever get. 3 But when you give to someone in need, don't let your left hand know what your right hand is doing. 4 Give your gifts in private, and your Father, who sees everything, will reward you.

19 "Don't store up treasures here on earth, where moths eat them and rust destroys them, and where thieves break in and steal. 20 Store your treasures in heaven, where moths and rust cannot destroy, and thieves do not break in and steal. 21 Wherever your treasure is, there the desires of your heart will also be."

1 Timothy 6:17-19

Teach those who are rich in this world not to be proud and not to trust in their money, which is so unreliable. Their trust should be in God, who richly gives us all we need for our enjoyment. 18 Tell them to use their money to do good. They should be rich in good works and generous to those in need, always being ready to share with others. 19 By doing this they will be storing up their treasure as a good foundation for the future so that they may experience true life.

Discipleship questions:

- In what ways are you generous with your resources? In what ways are you not?

- What is your internal attitude when you are faced with the prospect of giving?

- Since we all have a limited amount of time and resources, how do you decide where to invest what you have?

- What principles do you follow for practicing wisdom in giving?

- When it comes to giving of your money and resources, in what areas do you need to grow?

Make a budget:

Sit down with a sheet of paper and make two columns. In one column, write down all the sources of income you have in the course of an average month. In the other column, write down all of your standard monthly expenses (rent, gas, food, giving, etc.). What do you notice about how you spend your money? What do you notice about your priorities?

Action steps:

- **In light of our discussion, what is God asking you to do?**

- **How will you obey his prompting?**

- **When will you do it?**

- **Who will help you?**

- **With whom will you share what you have learned before we meet again?**

IV. Showing hospitality without favoritism

Key question: *How are you showing hospitality?*

People are often surprised to find hospitality as a part of generosity. Too often, we think of generosity as simply giving money. Such a narrow definition guts generosity of most of its life. Generosity begins with an impulse of the heart to invite. We invite people into our lives, to share our food, our space, and our time with us.

Remember too that hospitality isn't only for our friends. Hospitality means taking in the stranger and providing for practical needs. It does not depend on having a large or lavish home. It does not depend on our cooking skills. It does not depend on having spotlessly clean living quarters. Often people find simplicity more comfortable and authentic anyway. After all, when we invite others into our home, we are inviting into our lives... warts and all.

Meditation

"It's not how much we give but how much love we put into giving."
— **Mother Teresa**

How can we practice hospitality in simple ways? We can invite someone for coffee. We can bring a meal to the sick. We can invite those that others don't invite. We can extend a lunch-hour invitation to a coworker. We can throw a party. Although the classic means of inviting someone over to your home for dinner is wonderful, it's hardly the only way of showing hospitality. As you engage in this study with a few other people, consider some means of hospitality that would work well in your particular situation and context.

Brainstorm

List as many different ways of showing hospitality as you can. Consider the word "invitation." What can you invite people to?

This week read and reflect daily on the scripture below. Open a natural flow of conversational prayer with the Holy Spirit as you meditate on the scriptures, inviting him to reveal himself to you. Then gather with those who journey alongside you and interact over the discipleship questions.

Matthew 5:46-47

"If you love only those who love you, what reward is there for that? Even corrupt tax collectors do that much. 47 If you are kind only to your friends, how are you different from anyone else? Even pagans do that."

Matthew 22:1-10

Jesus also told them other parables. He said, 2 "The Kingdom of Heaven can be illustrated by the story of a king who prepared a great wedding feast for his son. 3 When the banquet was ready, he sent his servants to notify those who were invited. But they all refused to come!

4 "So he sent other servants to tell them, 'The feast has been prepared. The bulls and fattened cattle have been killed, and everything is ready. Come to the banquet!' 5 But the guests he had invited ignored them and went their own way, one to his farm, another to his business. 6 Others seized his messengers and insulted them and killed them.

7 "The king was furious, and he sent out his army to destroy the murderers and burn their town. 8 And he said to his servants, 'The wedding feast is ready, and the guests I invited aren't worthy of the honor. 9 Now go out to the street corners and invite everyone you see.' 10 So the servants brought in everyone they could find, good and bad alike, and the banquet hall was filled with guests."

Hebrews 13:1-3

Keep on loving each other as brothers and sisters. 2 Don't forget to show hospitality to strangers, for some who have done this have entertained angels without realizing it! 3 Remember those in prison, as if you were there yourself. Remember also those being mistreated, as if you felt their pain in your own bodies.

1 Peter 4:8-10

Most important of all, continue to show deep love for each other, for love covers a multitude of sins. 9 Cheerfully share your home with those who need a meal or a place to stay. 10 God has given each of you a gift from his great variety of spiritual gifts. Use them well to serve one another.

3 John 1:5-11

Dear friend, you are faithful in what you are doing for the brothers and sisters, even though they are strangers to you. 6 They have told the church about your love. Please send them on their way in a manner that honors God. 7 It was for the sake of the Name that they went out, receiving no help from the pagans. 8 We ought therefore to show hospitality to such people so that we may work together for the truth.

9 I wrote to the church, but Diotrephes, who loves to be first, will not welcome us. 10 So when I come, I will call attention to what he is doing, spreading malicious nonsense about us. Not satisfied with that, he even refuses to welcome other believers. He also stops those who want to do so and puts them out of the church.

11 Dear friend, do not imitate what is evil but what is good. (NIV)

Discipleship questions:

- What does the word "hospitality" mean to you?

- How do you see it used in these scriptures?

- Tell about a time when you were intentional about showing hospitality. What happened?

- When is a time when you experienced someone else's hospitality? What was that like?

- What might hospitality look like in our culture?

Action steps:

- **In light of our discussion, what is God asking you to do?**

- **How will you obey his prompting?**

- **When will you do it?**

- **Who will help you?**

- **With whom will you share what you have learned before we meet again?**

V. Living out your God-given calling

Key question: *How are you living out your God-given calling?*

"Calling" can be such an intimidating word. How are we to know something as momentous as our calling, much less live it out? Not everyone gets blinded by the light like the Apostle Paul was at the onset of his ministry. However, everyone does have a calling. Your calling can be raising good children. It can be your Thursday night ministry to those in prison that you do in addition to your ordinary day job. It can be teaching 3rd grade. We all have individual callings... but taken together with the callings of others they add up to something momentous. God asks each of us to do our part in his mission. That is calling.

Meditation

"Success is finding out what God wants you to do and doing it."

— **Sam Logan**

For those of us not blinded by the light like the Apostle Paul, calling can even be something we stumble into (or so it seems to us). Very few of us know what we want to be when we grow up. Instead, we start doing something, change directions, learn things along the way, and eventually land somewhere we never expected. That doesn't mean it's not our calling. If we are faithful in moving forward—even when we aren't sure where we are going—God will be faithful in guiding us where he wants us to go.

Paint a picture

Come up with an image in your mind that represents "calling" to you. What do you see? How would you articulate it?

This week read and reflect daily on the scripture below. Open a natural flow of conversational prayer with the Holy Spirit as you meditate on the scriptures, inviting him to reveal himself to you. Then gather with those who journey alongside you and interact over the discipleship questions.

Ephesians 2:10

For we are God's masterpiece. He has created us anew in Christ Jesus, so we can do the good things he planned for us long ago.

Ephesians 4:1-10

Therefore I, a prisoner for serving the Lord, beg you to lead a life worthy of your calling, for you have been called by God. 2 Always be humble and gentle. Be patient with each other, making allowance for each other's faults because of your love. 3 Make every effort to keep yourselves united in the Spirit, binding yourselves together with peace. 4 For there is one body and one Spirit, just as you have been called to one glorious hope for the future. 5 There is one Lord, one faith, one baptism, 6 and one God and Father, who is over all and in all and living through all.

7 However, he has given each one of us a special gift through the generosity of Christ. 8 That is why the Scriptures say,

"When he ascended to the heights,
he led a crowd of captives
and gave gifts to his people."

9 Notice that it says "he ascended." This clearly means that Christ also descended to our lowly world. 10 And the same one who descended is the one who ascended higher than all the heavens, so that he might fill the entire universe with himself.

Micah 6:8

No, O people, the Lord has told you what is good,
and this is what he requires of you:
to do what is right, to love mercy,
and to walk humbly with your God.

Discipleship questions:

- **How do you understand your calling?**

- **How has that become clear so far?**

- **What lies get in the way of you embracing your calling?**

- **If you are not sure of your specific calling, what are some steps you could take that may shed some light on your path?**

- **How can you be faithful with what you do know God is calling you to do?**

Action steps:

- In light of our discussion, what is God asking you to do?

- How will you obey his prompting?

- When will you do it?

- Who will help you?

- With whom will you share what you have learned before we meet again?

Disciplemaking

Making more and better followers of Jesus
by living the Great Commission

I. Engaging in spiritual conversations with those who are not yet followers of Jesus

Key question: *Who are you engaging in spiritual conversations with?*

One of the reasons sharing our faith gets a bad rap is that we are all talk and no listening. No matter what the topic of conversation is, no one enjoys engaging in discussion with someone who talks the whole time without asking questions of the other person and listening to their answers. It's just basic manners.

Engaging with others through listening and asking questions—and having that same attention returned to us—is an integral part of people's spiritual journey. Someone else asking us thought provoking questions and listening to our answers helps us engage with the ideas in a way we never could by receiving a lecture. This is simply a part of how God has wired us to learn.

As we are sent out into the world to make disciples, we need to engage in numerous conversations along the course of a relationship. It's not one high-stakes meeting where we need to make all the points we want to make. It's a series of conversations where we ask questions and really listen to the answers. And in real conversations, we recognize that not everyone always agrees with us. That's natural. We need to respect the differences and not engage in coercion or cut off the relationship because of disagreements. We can share our perspectives, but we need to recognize that not everyone will agree with us. That's okay—God is still at work in ways we don't understand. Our part is simply to remain faithful in continuing to engage in faith conversations marked by respect.

 Meditation

"Success is the ability to go from one failure to another with no loss of enthusiasm."

— Sir Winston Churchill

Questions:

Brainstorm some good, thought-provoking questions that you can ask others when the opportunity arises. Here are a few to get you started:
- What were you taught about God growing up?
- How have you explained death (of, say, a grandparent) to your children?
- What do you find meaningful about your work?

This week read and reflect daily on the scripture below. Open a natural flow of conversational prayer with the Holy Spirit as you meditate on the scriptures, inviting him to reveal himself to you. Then gather with those who journey alongside you and interact over the discipleship questions.

John 4:1-26

Jesus knew the Pharisees had heard that he was baptizing and making more disciples than John 2 (though Jesus himself didn't baptize them—his disciples did). 3 So he left Judea and returned to Galilee.

4 He had to go through Samaria on the way. 5 Eventually he came to the Samaritan village of Sychar, near the field that Jacob gave to his son Joseph. 6 Jacob's well was there; and Jesus, tired from the long walk, sat wearily beside the well about noontime. 7 Soon a Samaritan woman came to draw water, and Jesus said to her, "Please give me a drink." 8 He was alone at the time because his disciples had gone into the village to buy some food.

9 The woman was surprised, for Jews refuse to have anything to do with Samaritans. She said to Jesus, "You are a Jew, and I am a Samaritan woman. Why are you asking me for a drink?"

10 Jesus replied, "If you only knew the gift God has for you and who you are speaking to, you would ask me, and I would give you living water."

11 "But sir, you don't have a rope or a bucket," she said, "and this well is very deep. Where would you get this living water?

2 And besides, do you think you're greater than our ancestor Jacob, who gave us this well? How can you offer better water than he and his sons and his animals enjoyed?"

13 Jesus replied, "Anyone who drinks this water will soon become thirsty again. 14 But those who drink the water I give will never be thirsty again. It becomes a fresh, bubbling spring within them, giving them eternal life."

15 "Please, sir," the woman said, "give me this water! Then I'll never be thirsty again, and I won't have to come here to get water."

16 "Go and get your husband," Jesus told her.

17 "I don't have a husband," the woman replied.

Jesus said, "You're right! You don't have a husband— 18 for you have had five husbands, and you aren't even married to the man you're living with now. You certainly spoke the truth!"

19 "Sir," the woman said, "you must be a prophet. 20 So tell me, why is it that you Jews insist that Jerusalem is the only place of worship, while we Samaritans claim it is here at Mount Gerizim, where our ancestors worshipped?"

21 Jesus replied, "Believe me, dear woman, the time is coming when it will no longer matter whether you worship the Father on this mountain or in Jerusalem. 22 You Samaritans know very little about the one you worship, while we Jews know all about him, for salvation comes through the Jews. 23 But the time is coming—indeed it's here now—when true worshipers will worship the Father in spirit and in truth. The Father is looking for those who will worship him that way. 24 For God is Spirit, so those who worship him must worship in spirit and in truth."

25 The woman said, "I know the Messiah is coming—the one who is called Christ. When he comes, he will explain everything to us."

26 Then Jesus told her, "I Am the Messiah!"

Discipleship questions:

- How curious are you about the beliefs of others?

- Describe the last time you asked questions about someone's spiritual journey and listened without injecting your own opinion?

- What are the challenges of listening?

- How have people responded when you have listened?

- Where have you sensed the Holy Spirit at work as they've talked?

Action steps:

- **In light of our discussion, what is God asking you to do?**

- **How will you obey his prompting?**

- **When will you do it?**

- **Who will help you?**

- **With whom will you share what you have learned before we meet again?**

II. Explaining the good news and the way of Jesus

Key question: *How would you explain the good news of Jesus in a few simple sentences?*

Meditation

"Make everything as simple as possible, but not simpler."

— **Albert Einstein**

A very significant part of what Jesus told us to do was to pass the gospel message on to others. That's disciplemaking at the heart of the great commission. Passing on the gospel to others takes place in two parts: 1) having a clear understanding of the basic essentials of what the gospel is, and 2) deciding how best to communicate to others so they too will gain that understanding of the essentials. For example, Jesus used many agrarian and fishing examples, as they reflected the culture of the people he was trying to reach. How might we use modern day examples to explain to others the gospel?

Meditation

"I believe in Christianity as I believe that the sun has risen: not only because I see it, but because by it I see everything else."

— **C.S. Lewis**

This week read and reflect daily on the scripture on the next page. Open a natural flow of conversational prayer with the Holy Spirit as you meditate on the scriptures, inviting him to reveal himself to you. Then gather with those who journey alongside you and interact over the discipleship questions.

Psalm 34:8

> *Taste and see that the Lord is good.*
> *Oh, the joys of those who take refuge in him!*

Acts 18:24-28

> *Meanwhile, a Jew named Apollos, an eloquent speaker who knew the Scriptures well, had arrived in Ephesus from Alexandria in Egypt. 25 He had been taught the way of the Lord, and he taught others about Jesus with an enthusiastic spirit and with accuracy. However, he knew only about John's baptism. 26 When Priscilla and Aquila heard him preaching boldly in the synagogue, they took him aside and explained the way of God even more accurately.*

> *27 Apollos had been thinking about going to Achaia, and the brothers and sisters in Ephesus encouraged him to go. They wrote to the believers in Achaia, asking them to welcome him. When he arrived there, he proved to be of great benefit to those who, by God's grace, had believed. 28 He refuted the Jews with powerful arguments in public debate. Using the Scriptures, he explained to them that Jesus was the Messiah.*

Colossians 4:3-4

> *Pray for us, too, that God will give us many opportunities to speak about his mysterious plan concerning Christ. That is why I am here in chains. 4 Pray that I will proclaim this message as clearly as I should.*

Discipleship questions:

- Describe the gospel in under three minutes as you would to someone who doesn't already understand it.

- What do you understand to be the basic essentials of the gospel?

- Who do you know who needs to consider those essentials?

- How can you best invite that person to do so?

- How can the decision to follow Jesus be made more plain to people?

- Think of someone you are in relationship with. How can you invite them to follow Jesus in a way that will make sense to them?

- How will you balance your intellectual understanding of the essentials with experiential understanding?

Think of an image

Images — or word pictures — are used throughout scripture. A small seed growing into a large tree. An old wineskin breaking when filled with new wine. A vast field of wheat waiting to be harvested. When you consider the story of the gospel from within your own cultural context, what images come to mind? Choose one and write a paragraph about it.

Action steps:

- **In light of this, what is God asking you to do?**

- **How will you do this?**

- **When will you do this?**

- **Who will help you?**

III. Establishing new believers in a discipleship process

Key question: *Into what type of discipleship process are you establishing people?*

There are almost as many ways to disciple people as there are people. Yet if we leave the discipleship process completely wide open, what tends to happen is nothing. A better practice is to establish a default option for discipleship—a discipleship engine, if you will—and allow people to make changes and adaptations as needed.

Some of these discipleship methods include Life Transformation Groups (LTGs), T for T, SOAP, coaching relationships, and even these Dimensions of Discipleship Guides you hold in your hands. Anything that provides some basic content and some format for processing that content alongside others can function as a discipleship engine.

The element of learning from one another is a non-negotiable in discipleship. We cannot learn to become more like Jesus and follow him more faithfully in isolation from others. It's simply not how we were designed as humans, and it certainly is not how Jesus established people in a discipleship process. We are all different parts of the same body and we all bring different gifts to the table. Because of this relational dynamic, no one can disciple another person alone. The full Body of Christ is needed. We can learn things from one another that we cannot learn on our own or from just one other person.

 Meditation

"Learn from the mistakes of others. You can't live long enough to make them all yourself."

— **Eleanor Roosevelt**

This week read and reflect daily on the scripture on the next page. Open a natural flow of conversational prayer with the Holy Spirit as you meditate on the scriptures, inviting him to reveal himself to you. Then gather with those who journey alongside you and interact over the discipleship questions.

Colossians 3:12-17

Since God chose you to be the holy people he loves, you must clothe yourselves with tenderhearted mercy, kindness, humility, gentleness, and patience. 13 Make allowance for each other's faults, and forgive anyone who offends you. Remember, the Lord forgave you, so you must forgive others. 14 Above all, clothe yourselves with love, which binds us all together in perfect harmony. 15 And let the peace that comes from Christ rule in your hearts. For as members of one body you are called to live in peace. And always be thankful.

16 Let the message about Christ, in all its richness, fill your lives. Teach and counsel each other with all the wisdom he gives. Sing psalms and hymns and spiritual songs to God with thankful hearts. 17 And whatever you do or say, do it as a representative of the Lord Jesus, giving thanks through him to God the Father.

2 Timothy 1:13-14

Hold on to the pattern of wholesome teaching you learned from me—a pattern shaped by the faith and love that you have in Christ Jesus. 14 Through the power of the Holy Spirit who lives within us, carefully guard the precious truth that has been entrusted to you.

Matthew 11:28-30

Then Jesus said, "Come to me, all of you who are weary and carry heavy burdens, and I will give you rest. 29 Take my yoke upon you. Let me teach you, because I am humble and gentle at heart, and you will find rest for your souls. 30 For my yoke is easy to bear, and the burden I give you is light."

Discipleship questions:

- What are the essential hallmarks of a healthy discipleship relationship? List as many as you can think of.

- Who are you currently discipling?

- How does that relationship incorporate the elements you listed?

- Which elements are present and which are missing or incomplete?

- At what point will you challenge the person you are discipling to begin discipling someone else?

- How will you prepare him or her for that responsibility?

Review your options

What disciplemaking engines are you aware of? Review them and decide which would best fit in your context. Then try it out yourself. What works well? What adjustments might need to be made?

Action steps:

- **In light of our discussion, what is God asking you to do?**

- **How will you obey his prompting?**

- **When will you do it?**

- **Who will help you?**

- **With whom will you share what you have learned before we meet again?**

IV. Connecting people with a faith community

Key question: *How can you connect new believers with a faith community?*

We need one another. Christianity is not a go-it-alone faith. The way God has set up the church from the beginning is that we are to live out our faith from within a context of community. A new believer must have fellowship of some kind with other believers. That community provides the means of encouragement, challenging, learning, and prayer. Therefore, every time a new believer comes to the faith, they must be connected to the larger body of Christ.

However, there is a dilemma that taking someone out of their natural network of relationships and surrounding them with Christians can block the continuing path of others coming to faith through that network of relationships. So at the same time that you connect new believers with the body, you also need to ensure that they remain connected to their natural network of friends, family, and co-workers.

Meditation

"Every time there is a new convert, you have discovered an elbow, a kneecap, or a nose. The assumption is that the rest of the body must be nearby and a church will emerge through evangelizing the new convert's network of relationships. Through any one person, you can find the seeds of a new church."

— **Robert E. Logan,** *Be Fruitful and Multiply*

This week read and reflect daily on the scripture on the next page. Open a natural flow of conversational prayer with the Holy Spirit as you meditate on the scriptures, inviting him to reveal himself to you. Then gather with those who journey alongside you and interact over the discipleship questions.

Acts 2:42-47

All the believers devoted themselves to the apostles' teaching, and to fellowship, and to sharing in meals (including the Lord's Supper), and to prayer.

43 A deep sense of awe came over them all, and the apostles performed many miraculous signs and wonders. 44 And all the believers met together in one place and shared everything they had. 45 They sold their property and possessions and shared the money with those in need. 46 They worshipped together at the Temple each day, met in homes for the Lord's Supper, and shared their meals with great joy and generosity— 47 all the while praising God and enjoying the goodwill of all the people. And each day the Lord added to their fellowship those who were being saved.

Acts 16:14-15

One of them was Lydia from Thyatira, a merchant of expensive purple cloth, who worshipped God. As she listened to us, the Lord opened her heart, and she accepted what Paul was saying. 15 She and her household were baptized, and she asked us to be her guests. "If you agree that I am a true believer in the Lord," she said, "come and stay at my home." And she urged us until we agreed.

Acts 16:31-34

They replied, "Believe in the Lord Jesus and you will be saved, along with everyone in your household." 32 And they shared the word of the Lord with him and with all who lived in his household. 33 Even at that hour of the night, the jailer cared for them and washed their wounds. Then he and everyone in his household were immediately baptized. 34 He brought them into his house and set a meal before them, and he and his entire household rejoiced because they all believed in God.

Discipleship questions:

- When have you seen a new believer completely submerged into the church? What did that look like? What were the results?

- What are the risks of continuing with their existing network of relationships? What are the possible benefits?

- How can you take a both-and approach?

- What do new believers need from other believers? How can you ensure that is provided?

Action steps:

- **In light of our discussion, what is God asking you to do?**

- **How will you obey his prompting?**

- **When will you do it?**

- **Who will help you?**

- **With whom will you share what you have learned before we meet again?**

V. Helping new followers make more followers

Key question: *How are you helping new followers of Jesus make more followers of Jesus?*

You could make 100 followers of Jesus, yet if you don't help them go on to make other followers of Jesus, the long-term impact will be small. On the contrary, if you made three followers of Jesus and taught them all to make more followers, and they taught those they discipled to make more disciples, the long-term impact would be significant and far-reaching. Such is the power of multiplication over addition.

The personal impact on ourselves is equally significant. God calls us to pour out what he has poured out on us. Because we have been loved, we love. It's contagious. When God is at work in your life, you naturally have something to share with others. In turn, your sharing with others opens you up wider to the work God is doing within you. If we are in relationship with God, we have a story to tell... and that story was meant to be passed on from person to person to person through the generations.

 Meditation

"But how could you live and have no story to tell?"
— **Fyodor Dostoyevsky, *White Nights***

This week read and reflect daily on the scripture below. Open a natural flow of conversational prayer with the Holy Spirit as you meditate on the scriptures, inviting him to reveal himself to you. Then gather with those who journey alongside you and interact over the discipleship questions.

Acts 16:4-5

> *Then they went from town to town, instructing the believers to follow the decisions made by the apostles and elders in Jerusalem. 5 So the churches were strengthened in their faith and grew larger every day.*

Ephesians 4:11-13

Now these are the gifts Christ gave to the church: the apostles, the prophets, the evangelists, and the pastors and teachers. 12 Their responsibility is to equip God's people to do his work and build up the church, the body of Christ. 13 This will continue until we all come to such unity in our faith and knowledge of God's Son that we will be mature in the Lord, measuring up to the full and complete standard of Christ.

John 4:39-42

Many Samaritans from the village believed in Jesus because the woman had said, "He told me everything I ever did!" 40 When they came out to see him, they begged him to stay in their village. So he stayed for two days, 41 long enough for many more to hear his message and believe. 42 Then they said to the woman, "Now we believe, not just because of what you told us, but because we have heard him ourselves. Now we know that he is indeed the Savior of the world."

Deuteronomy 7:8-9

Rather, it was simply that the Lord loves you, and he was keeping the oath he had sworn to your ancestors. That is why the Lord rescued you with such a strong hand from your slavery and from the oppressive hand of Pharaoh, king of Egypt. 9 Understand, therefore, that the Lord your God is indeed God. He is the faithful God who keeps his covenant for a thousand generations and lavishes his unfailing love on those who love him and obey his commands.

 Meditation

"The greatest single cause of atheism in the world today is Christians: who acknowledge Jesus with their lips, walk out the door, and deny Him by their lifestyle. That is what an unbelieving world simply finds unbelievable."

— Brennan Manning

Discipleship questions:

- **What spiritual legacy do you hope to leave?**

- **How are you challenging those you are discipling to make more disciples?**

- **How will you ensure that disciplemaking covers multiple generations?**

- **How are you best equipped to not just make but multiply disciples?**

- **What is your vision for future generations of believers?**

- **What blessings can you pray on the next generation of leaders?**

Dollars and cents:

Suppose a father offers his two sons the choice of taking either one dollar a week for 52 weeks or one cent the first week and an amount each week for the next 51 one weeks that is double the previous week's amount. Which one would you choose?

The first choice would just be adding one dollar each week —that's linear growth. At the end of 52 weeks—he'd have $52. The second choice is multiplication—that's exponential growth. If one of the sons chooses this, at the end of the year he will have an unbelievable amount of money. In fact, his allowance in the last week (not the total amount accumulated over 52 weeks) would be $22,517,998,136,852.48. Initially the multiplication is slow, but don't let that deceive you. In the long run, addition never keeps pace with multiplication. Multiplication is explosive.

Action steps:

- **In light of our discussion, what is God asking you to do?**

- **How will you obey his prompting?**

- **When will you do it?**

- **Who will help you?**

- **With whom will you share what you have learned before we meet again?**

Personal Transformation

Changing your behaviors and attitudes because of your relationships with God and others

I. Actively engaging with God in the examination of your heart

Key question: *When and how are you setting aside time to reflect on your heart?*

Without taking the time to reflect on ourselves and our experiences, we can be exposed to great teachings and be a part of amazing experiences, yet not be transformed in any deep or meaningful way on a personal level. When we hear scripture, we need to reflect on it. When we do ministry, we need to consider how it is going and what we could do differently. When we experience God, we need to consider how that can change and mature us.

Meditation

"Love all God's creation, the whole and every grain of sand in it. Love every leaf, every ray of God's light. Love the animals, love the plants, love everything. If you love everything, you will perceive the divine mystery in things. Once you perceive it, you will begin to comprehend it better every day. And you will come at last to love the whole world with an all-embracing love."

— **Fyodor Dostoyevsky,** *The Brothers Karamazov*

What are the ways we can actively engage with God as we reflect? We can reflect in silence and prayer, listening for the voice of God and being open to the leading of his Spirit. We can discuss and pray together with others in the body of Christ, asking for their insights and perspectives. We can work with a coach, mentor or spiritual director who asks us questions to help us discern where God might be at work in our lives. Engaging in this study with a few other people can be a great first step toward deeper reflection.

> ### *Journal*
>
> Take some time alone and write or draw about these three questions: What have I been hearing from God lately? What am I learning from my experiences? Who might be able to speak into my life right now? Don't worry about getting the words just right—you are the only one who will be reading it—just say what you want to say.

This week read and reflect daily on the scripture below. Open a natural flow of conversational prayer with the Holy Spirit as you meditate on the scriptures, inviting him to reveal himself to you. Then gather with those who journey alongside you and interact over the discussion questions.

Colossians 3:1-17

Since you have been raised to new life with Christ, set your sights on the realities of heaven, where Christ sits in the place of honor at God's right hand. 2 Think about the things of heaven, not the things of earth. 3 For you died to this life, and your real life is hidden with Christ in God. 4 And when Christ, who is your life, is revealed to the whole world, you will share in all his glory.

5 So put to death the sinful, earthly things lurking within you. Have nothing to do with sexual immorality, impurity, lust, and evil desires. Don't be greedy, for a greedy person is an idolater, worshiping the things of this world. 6 Because of these sins, the anger of God is coming. 7 You used to do these things when your life was still part of this world. 8 But now is the time to get rid of anger, rage, malicious behavior, slander, and dirty language. 9 Don't lie to each other, for you have stripped off your old sinful nature and all its wicked deeds. 10 Put on your new nature, and be renewed as you learn to know your Creator and become like him. 11 In this new life, it doesn't matter if you are a Jew or a Gentile, circumcised or uncircumcised, barbaric, uncivilized, slave, or free. Christ is all that matters, and he lives in all of us.

12 Since God chose you to be the holy people he loves, you must clothe yourselves with tenderhearted mercy, kindness, humility, gentleness, and patience.

13 Make allowance for each other's faults, and forgive anyone who offends you. Remember, the Lord forgave you, so you must forgive others.

14 Above all, clothe yourselves with love, which binds us all together in perfect harmony. 15 And let the peace that comes from Christ rule in your hearts. For as members of one body you are called to live in peace. And always be thankful.

16 Let the message about Christ, in all its richness, fill your lives. Teach and counsel each other with all the wisdom he gives. Sing psalms and hymns and spiritual songs to God with thankful hearts. 17 And whatever you do or say, do it as a representative of the Lord Jesus, giving thanks through him to God the Father.

James 1:22-25

But don't just listen to God's word. You must do what it says. Otherwise, you are only fooling yourselves. 23 For if you listen to the word and don't obey, it is like glancing at your face in a mirror. 24 You see yourself, walk away, and forget what you look like. 25 But if you look carefully into the perfect law that sets you free, and if you do what it says and don't forget what you heard, then God will bless you for doing it.

Luke 18:9-14

Then Jesus told this story to some who had great confidence in their own righteousness and scorned everyone else: 10 "Two men went to the Temple to pray. One was a Pharisee, and the other was a despised tax collector. 11 The Pharisee stood by himself and prayed this prayer: 'I thank you, God, that I am not a sinner like everyone else. For I don't cheat, I don't sin, and I don't commit adultery. I'm certainly not like that tax collector! 12 I fast twice a week, and I give you a tenth of my income.'

13 "But the tax collector stood at a distance and dared not even lift his eyes to heaven as he prayed. Instead, he beat his chest in sorrow, saying, 'O God, be merciful to me, for I am a sinner.' 14 I tell you, this sinner, not the Pharisee, returned home justified before God. For those who exalt themselves will be humbled, and those who humble themselves will be exalted."

Discipleship questions:

- Describe a time when you intentionally set aside some time for reflection. How did you do that? What came of it?

- What are your impressions of the story of the tax collector and the Pharisee?

- When is a time when you really felt God speaking to you? How did he do that?

- What strategies have been most helpful in getting you to reflect? Which others might you want to try?

- What gets in the way of your reflecting? What steps might you take to overcome that barrier?

Action steps:

- **In light of our discussion, what is God asking you to do?**

- **How will you obey his prompting?**

- **When will you do it?**

- **Who will help you?**

- **With whom will you share what you have learned before we meet again?**

II. Cooperating with God's healing work in your life

Key question: *How are you cooperating with God's healing work in your life?*

God desires to do healing work in your life. It's not as if some people need healing and others don't. We all need healing in different ways, whether physical, emotional, relational, spiritual, or some other type of healing. We live in a broken world and we are broken people. We stand in need of God's healing, with nothing to offer him in return.

Yet with healing comes risk. We need to step forward and be willing to be healed. Not everyone who needs healing is willing to be healed. To recognize oneself in need of healing and to open oneself to the Spirit of God to do his work takes a great deal of courage and trust. It is not easy and it is not passive.

Meditation

"...and then the day came when the risk to remain tight, in a bud, became more painful than the risk it took to blossom..."

— **Elizabeth Appell**

We need to stand before God with empty hands and allow him to do his healing work in our lives. That might mean we need to forgive, to let go, to stay, to accept. We do not know what God may ask of us when we put ourselves in his hands. What we do know is that he desires us to become our best selves, reflections of him, healed and whole.

Journal

In what ways do you need healing? Meditate on the broken areas in your life and consider what healing might look like. What would you need to let go of in order for God to heal that area of your life?

This week read and reflect daily on the scripture below. Open a natural flow of conversational prayer with the Holy Spirit as you meditate on the scriptures, inviting him to reveal himself to you. Then gather with those who journey alongside you and interact over the discussion questions.

John 5:1-9

Afterward Jesus returned to Jerusalem for one of the Jewish holy days. 2 Inside the city, near the Sheep Gate, was the pool of Bethesda, with five covered porches. 3 Crowds of sick people—blind, lame, or paralyzed—lay on the porches. 5 One of the men lying there had been sick for thirty-eight years. 6 When Jesus saw him and knew he had been ill for a long time, he asked him, "Would you like to get well?"

7 "I can't, sir," the sick man said, "for I have no one to put me into the pool when the water bubbles up. Someone else always gets there ahead of me."

8 Jesus told him, "Stand up, pick up your mat, and walk!"

9 Instantly, the man was healed! He rolled up his sleeping mat and began walking!

Matthew 4:23-24

Jesus traveled throughout the region of Galilee, teaching in the synagogues and announcing the Good News about the Kingdom. And he healed every kind of disease and illness. 24 News about him spread as far as Syria, and people soon began bringing to him all who were sick. And whatever their sickness or disease, or if they were demon possessed or epileptic or paralyzed—he healed them all.

Matthew 9:10-13

Later, Matthew invited Jesus and his disciples to his home as dinner guests, along with many tax collectors and other disreputable sinners. 11 But when the Pharisees saw this, they asked his disciples, "Why does your teacher eat with such scum?"

12 When Jesus heard this, he said, "Healthy people don't need a doctor—sick people do." 13 Then he added, "Now go and learn the meaning of this Scripture: 'I want you to show mercy, not offer sacrifices.' For I have come to call not those who think they are righteous, but those who know they are sinners."

James 5:16

Confess your sins to each other and pray for each other so that you may be healed. The earnest prayer of a righteous person has great power and produces wonderful results.

1 Peter 2:24-25

He personally carried our sins
* in his body on the cross*
so that we can be dead to sin
* and live for what is right.*
By his wounds
* you are healed.*
25 Once you were like sheep
* who wandered away.*
But now you have turned to your Shepherd,
* the Guardian of your souls.*

Meditation

"Only people who are capable of loving strongly can also suffer great sorrow, but this same necessity of loving serves to counteract their grief and heals them."

— Leo Tolstoy

Discipleship questions:

- ✎ **What areas of your life stand in need of healing?**

- ✎ **Are you willing to be healed?**

- ✎ **What will that healing require of you?**

- ✎ **What fears do you have around being healed?**

- ✎ **How might God be able to use you if you cooperate with his healing work in your life?**

Action steps:

- In light of our discussion, what is God asking you to do?

- How will you obey his prompting?

- When will you do it?

- Who will help you?

- With whom will you share what you have learned before we meet again?

III. Processing feedback and input from others

Key question: *How are you requesting and processing constructive input from others?*

How do we know if we're doing well? In certain fields such as math, there is a clearly right answer and clearly wrong answers. In other fields, such as spirituality, relationships, and personal transformation, it's not quite so clear. There are different perspectives to take into account and different goals that may—or may not—be agreed upon. It would be great if we had some built-in way to determine how we're doing, but that's not the way it works. Like many other things, God has set this up organically in such a way that we need each other.

Meditation

"Computers are great because when you're working with them you get immediate results that let you know if your program works. It's feedback you don't get from many other things."

— Bill Gates

We need to find ways to open ourselves up to constructive input from others. Sometimes people, both inside and outside the church, will give us unsolicited feedback. In those cases, we need to evaluate the feedback to see if it is constructive and helpful. If so, we need to reflect on it and find ways to incorporate it into our lives. If not, we are free to discard it. Yet most of the time people will not give uninvited feedback. We need to ask for it. We can often find a great deal of useful feedback simply by asking people we trust who are in a position to give helpful feedback.

This week read and reflect daily on the scripture on the next page. Open a natural flow of conversational prayer with the Holy Spirit as you meditate on the scriptures, inviting him to reveal himself to you. Then gather with those who journey alongside you and interact over the discussion questions.

Ecclesiastes 4:9-13

Two people are better off than one, for they can help each other succeed. 10 If one person falls, the other can reach out and help. But someone who falls alone is in real trouble. 11 Likewise, two people lying close together can keep each other warm. But how can one be warm alone? 12 A person standing alone can be attacked and defeated, but two can stand back-to-back and conquer. Three are even better, for a triple-braided cord is not easily broken. 13 It is better to be a poor but wise youth than an old and foolish king who refuses all advice.

Galatians 2:11-14

But when Peter came to Antioch, I had to oppose him to his face, for what he did was very wrong. 12 When he first arrived, he ate with the Gentile believers, who were not circumcised. But afterward, when some friends of James came, Peter wouldn't eat with the Gentiles anymore. He was afraid of criticism from these people who insisted on the necessity of circumcision. 13 As a result, other Jewish believers followed Peter's hypocrisy, and even Barnabas was led astray by their hypocrisy.

14 When I saw that they were not following the truth of the gospel message, I said to Peter in front of all the others, "Since you, a Jew by birth, have discarded the Jewish laws and are living like a Gentile, why are you now trying to make these Gentiles follow the Jewish traditions?

Proverbs

*The godly give good advice to their friends;
the wicked lead them astray. (12:26)*

*Pride leads to conflict;
those who take advice are wise. (13:10)*

*Plans go wrong for lack of advice;
many advisers bring success. (15:22)*

*Timely advice is lovely,
like golden apples in a silver basket. (25:11)*

Discipleship questions:

- Who has given you unsolicited feedback that was constructive and helpful? What did you do with that feedback?

- Who have you asked for feedback lately? Who might be in a good position to give it?

- How can you tell the difference between constructive and destructive feedback?

- What makes it difficult for you to ask for and receive feedback? What steps might you take to address those roadblocks?

Action steps:

- In light of our discussion, what is God asking you to do?

- How will you obey his prompting?

- When will you do it?

- Who will help you?

- With whom will you share what you have learned before we meet again?

IV. Living out new priorities and changed behavior

Key question: *How are you living out new priorities and changed behavior?*

The whole point of the gospel isn't to get us to think different things or even to do different things... it's to help us become different. Through his presence, God shapes us more and more into the unique person we were meant to be. We are transformed by our encounter with God, and that transformation shows itself in new priorities and new actions. We live out the change that God has worked within us.

 Meditation

> "Fairy tales do not tell children the dragons exist. Children already know that dragons exist. Fairy tales tell children the dragons can be killed."
>
> **— G.K. Chesterton**

This week read and reflect daily on the scripture below. Open a natural flow of conversational prayer with the Holy Spirit as you meditate on the scriptures, inviting him to reveal himself to you. Then gather with those who journey alongside you and interact over the discussion questions.

Acts 9:1-22

Meanwhile, Saul was uttering threats with every breath and was eager to kill the Lord's followers. So he went to the high priest. 2 He requested letters addressed to the synagogues in Damascus, asking for their cooperation in the arrest of any followers of the Way he found there. He wanted to bring them—both men and women—back to Jerusalem in chains.

3 As he was approaching Damascus on this mission, a light from heaven suddenly shone down around him. 4 He fell to the ground and heard a voice saying to him, "Saul! Saul! Why are you persecuting me?"

5 "Who are you, lord?" Saul asked.

And the voice replied, "I am Jesus, the one you are persecuting!

6 Now get up and go into the city, and you will be told what you must do."

7 The men with Saul stood speechless, for they heard the sound of someone's voice but saw no one! 8 Saul picked himself up off the ground, but when he opened his eyes he was blind. So his companions led him by the hand to Damascus. 9 He remained there blind for three days and did not eat or drink.

10 Now there was a believer in Damascus named Ananias. The Lord spoke to him in a vision, calling, "Ananias!"

"Yes, Lord!" he replied.

11 The Lord said, "Go over to Straight Street, to the house of Judas. When you get there, ask for a man from Tarsus named Saul. He is praying to me right now. 12 I have shown him a vision of a man named Ananias coming in and laying hands on him so he can see again."

13 "But Lord," exclaimed Ananias, "I've heard many people talk about the terrible things this man has done to the believers in Jerusalem! 14 And he is authorized by the leading priests to arrest everyone who calls upon your name."

15 But the Lord said, "Go, for Saul is my chosen instrument to take my message to the Gentiles and to kings, as well as to the people of Israel. 16 And I will show him how much he must suffer for my name's sake."

17 So Ananias went and found Saul. He laid his hands on him and said, "Brother Saul, the Lord Jesus, who appeared to you on the road, has sent me so that you might regain your sight and be filled with the Holy Spirit." 18 Instantly something like scales fell from Saul's eyes, and he regained his sight. Then he got up and was baptized. 19 Afterward he ate some food and regained his strength.

Saul stayed with the believers in Damascus for a few days. 20 And immediately he began preaching about Jesus in the synagogues, saying, "He is indeed the Son of God!"

21 All who heard him were amazed. "Isn't this the same man who caused such devastation among Jesus' followers in Jerusalem?" they asked. "And didn't he come here to arrest them and take them in chains to the leading priests?"

22 Saul's preaching became more and more powerful, and the Jews in Damascus couldn't refute his proofs that Jesus was indeed the Messiah.

Mark 5:1-20

So they arrived at the other side of the lake, in the region of the Gerasenes. 2 When Jesus climbed out of the boat, a man possessed by an evil spirit came out from the tombs to meet him. 3 This man lived in the burial caves and could no longer be restrained, even with a chain. 4 Whenever he was put into chains and shackles—as he often was—he snapped the chains from his wrists and smashed the shackles. No one was strong enough to subdue him. 5 Day and night he wandered among the burial caves and in the hills, howling and cutting himself with sharp stones.

6 When Jesus was still some distance away, the man saw him, ran to meet him, and bowed low before him. 7 With a shriek, he screamed, "Why are you interfering with me, Jesus, Son of the Most High God? In the name of God, I beg you, don't torture me!" 8 For Jesus had already said to the spirit, "Come out of the man, you evil spirit."

9 Then Jesus demanded, "What is your name?"

And he replied, "My name is Legion, because there are many of us inside this man." 10 Then the evil spirits begged him again and again not to send them to some distant place.

11 There happened to be a large herd of pigs feeding on the hillside nearby. 12 "Send us into those pigs," the spirits begged. "Let us enter them."

13 So Jesus gave them permission. The evil spirits came out of the man and entered the pigs, and the entire herd of about 2,000 pigs plunged down the steep hillside into the lake and drowned in the water.

14 The herdsmen fled to the nearby town and the surrounding countryside, spreading the news as they ran. People rushed out to see what had happened. 15 A crowd soon gathered around Jesus, and they saw the man who had been possessed by the legion of demons. He was sitting there fully clothed and perfectly sane, and they were all afraid. 16 Then those who had seen what happened told the others about the demon-possessed man and the pigs. 17 And the crowd began pleading with Jesus to go away and leave them alone.

18 As Jesus was getting into the boat, the man who had been demon possessed begged to go with him. 19 But Jesus said, "No, go home to your family, and tell them everything the Lord has done for you and how merciful he has been."

20 So the man started off to visit the Ten Towns of that region and began to proclaim the great things Jesus had done for him; and everyone was amazed at what he told them.

Discipleship questions:

- Describe a time in your life that you successfully changed a behavior or habit. What was it that enabled you to make that change?

- What motivates you?

- When have you had a true encounter with God? How did that change you?

- How would you like others to describe you? What needs to change in your life for that to be an accurate description?

Exercise:

Make a list of what you see as your priorities, and write each one on a separate sticky note. Make a list of the ways in which you spend your time, and write each one on a separate sticky note. Now put the notes in two columns on the wall or a whiteboard. How do items in the two lists align? Where do you see connections? What do you need to do more of in order to make your time reflect your priorities? What do you need to do less of?

 ## Meditation

"I'm a little pencil in the hand of a writing God, who is sending a love letter to the world."

— **Mother Teresa**

Action steps:

- In light of our discussion, what is God asking you to do?

- How will you obey his prompting?

- When will you do it?

- Who will help you?

- With whom will you share what you have learned before we meet again?

V. Increasingly bearing the fruit of the Spirit

Key question: *How are you growing in the fruit of the Spirit?*

As we are transformed, we should increasingly see evidence of the fruit of the Spirit in our lives. Where do we see love? Joy? Peace? What actions of ours can we point to that demonstrate patience? Kindness? Goodness? What evidence can we find of faithfulness? Gentleness? Self-control? The more we can see specific instances of these qualities in our lives, the more we know that the Spirit is truly doing his transformative work in our lives... because these qualities are the result of that work.

Christian Schwarz, in his book ***The 3 Colors of Love***, makes the case that there is only one fruit of the Spirit—Love—along with its 8 descriptors: joy, peace, patience, kindness, goodness, faithfulness, gentleness, and self-control. When you compare 1 Corinthians 13 and Galatians 5, you'll see there's a great deal of correlation. Whether you see the fruit of the Spirit as 9 or 1, the issue is that we need to grow. We need to assess where we're at and how to deepen character. Stagnation is not a viable option.

 Meditation

> "Patience is waiting. Not passively waiting. That is laziness. But to keep going when the going is hard and slow—that is patience."
>
> **— Anonymous**

This week read and reflect daily on the scripture on the next page. Open a natural flow of conversational prayer with the Holy Spirit as you meditate on the scriptures, inviting him to reveal himself to you. Then gather with those who journey alongside you and interact over the discussion questions.

Galatians 5:13-26

For you have been called to live in freedom, my brothers and sisters. But don't use your freedom to satisfy your sinful nature. Instead, use your freedom to serve one another in love. 14 For the whole law can be summed up in this one command: "Love your neighbor as yourself." 15 But if you are always biting and devouring one another, watch out! Beware of destroying one another.

16 So I say, let the Holy Spirit guide your lives. Then you won't be doing what your sinful nature craves. 17 The sinful nature wants to do evil, which is just the opposite of what the Spirit wants. And the Spirit gives us desires that are the opposite of what the sinful nature desires. These two forces are constantly fighting each other, so you are not free to carry out your good intentions. 18 But when you are directed by the Spirit, you are not under obligation to the law of Moses.

19 When you follow the desires of your sinful nature, the results are very clear: sexual immorality, impurity, lustful pleasures, 20 idolatry, sorcery, hostility, quarreling, jealousy, outbursts of anger, selfish ambition, dissension, division, 21 envy, drunkenness, wild parties, and other sins like these. Let me tell you again, as I have before, that anyone living that sort of life will not inherit the Kingdom of God.

22 But the Holy Spirit produces this kind of fruit in our lives: love, joy, peace, patience, kindness, goodness, faithfulness, 23 gentleness, and self-control. There is no law against these things!

24 Those who belong to Christ Jesus have nailed the passions and desires of their sinful nature to his cross and crucified them there. 25 Since we are living by the Spirit, let us follow the Spirit's leading in every part of our lives. 26 Let us not become conceited, or provoke one another, or be jealous of one another.

I Corinthians 13:4-7

Love is patient and kind. Love is not jealous or boastful or proud 5 or rude. It does not demand its own way. It is not irritable, and it keeps no record of being wronged. 6 It does not rejoice about injustice but rejoices whenever the truth wins out. 7 Love never gives up, never loses faith, is always hopeful, and endures through every circumstance.

Discipleship questions:

- **If someone invisible were to follow you around for a week, observing your behavior, what qualities do you think they might use to describe you?**

- **What character qualities do you consider your strengths? What character qualities do you consider your weaknesses?**

- **How have you approached improving your weaknesses?**

- **What are your thoughts on Christian Schwarz's interpretation of the fruit of the Spirit (described above)? How might that perspective assist you in your growth?**

- **What practices might help you increasingly bear the fruit of the Spirit?**

Journal the fruit of the Spirit

Dedicate one page to each of the nine fruits of the Spirit. Underneath each, write as many examples as you can of times you experienced each of those qualities... either by demonstrating them yourself or by receiving them from others.

Action steps:

- In light of our discussion, what is God asking you to do?

- How will you obey his prompting?

- When will you do it?

- Who will help you?

- With whom will you share what you have learned before we meet again?

Authentic Relationships

Engaging with other people in ways that
reflect the heart of God toward them

I. Showing respect for all people

Key question: *How are you showing respect for all people? How can you grow in that?*

We treat people with respect because they are created in the image of God. Every single human being on the earth—from beggars on the street to kings and rulers, young and old, healthy and sick, people we like and people we don't. We are all created in the image of God and deserving of basic respect.

 Meditation

"You can safely assume you've created God in your own image when it turns out that God hates all the same people you do."

— **Anne Lamott, Traveling Mercies**

How does that respect show? In many, many different ways, depending on the needs and on the relationship you have with the person: treating others with kindness, being honest, doing no harm, respecting the opinions of others even when you disagree, practicing generosity, taking time, showing patience. The list of possibilities is as long as scripture itself.

Prayer and journaling

Who do you have the most trouble respecting? You can think of individuals or groups of people. (Consider economic status, race, culture, education, religion, sexual orientation, status, life choices, etc.) What is it that gets in the way of respect? What steps can you take to address that? As a first step, set aside half an hour to pray for people you have a tough time respecting. Journal about that experience afterwards.

This week read and reflect daily on the scripture below. Open a natural flow of conversational prayer with the Holy Spirit as you meditate on the scriptures, inviting him to reveal himself to you. Then gather with those who journey alongside you and interact over the discipleship questions.

Genesis 1:26-27

Then God said, "Let us make human beings in our image, to be like us. They will reign over the fish in the sea, the birds in the sky, the livestock, all the wild animals on the earth, and the small animals that scurry along the ground."

27 So God created human beings in his own image.
    In the image of God he created them;
    male and female he created them.

Of note

Namaste (greeting, from the Sanskrit and Hindi): I see God in you

Genesis 33:10-11

But Jacob insisted, "No, if I have found favor with you, please accept this gift from me. And what a relief to see your friendly smile. It is like seeing the face of God! 11 Please take this gift I have brought you, for God has been very gracious to me. I have more than enough." And because Jacob insisted, Esau finally accepted the gift.

James 2:1-13

My dear brothers and sisters, how can you claim to have faith in our glorious Lord Jesus Christ if you favor some people over others?

2 For example, suppose someone comes into your meeting dressed in fancy clothes and expensive jewelry, and another comes in who is poor and dressed in dirty clothes. 3 If you give special attention and a good seat to the rich person, but you say to the poor one, "You can stand over there, or else sit on the floor"— well, 4 doesn't this discrimination show that your judgments are guided by evil motives?

5 Listen to me, dear brothers and sisters. Hasn't God chosen the poor in this world to be rich in faith? Aren't they the ones who will inherit the Kingdom he promised to those who love him? 6 But you dishonor the poor! Isn't it the rich who oppress you and drag you into court? 7 Aren't they the ones who slander Jesus Christ, whose noble name you bear?

8 Yes indeed, it is good when you obey the royal law as found in the Scriptures: "Love your neighbor as yourself." 9 But if you favor some people over others, you are committing a sin. You are guilty of breaking the law.

10 For the person who keeps all of the laws except one is as guilty as a person who has broken all of God's laws. 11 For the same God who said, "You must not commit adultery," also said, "You must not murder." So if you murder someone but do not commit adultery, you have still broken the law.

12 So whatever you say or whatever you do, remember that you will be judged by the law that sets you free. 13 There will be no mercy for those who have not shown mercy to others. But if you have been merciful, God will be merciful when he judges you.

Discipleship questions:

- **When have you seen God in someone else? What has that looked like?**

- **Where do you see the image of God in those who do not yet follow Jesus?**

- **How can you more intentionally seek to see the image of God in people?**

- **Who do you know right now who needs to believe that the image of God resides in them?**

- **What are ways you show respect? What are ways you indicate when you do not respect people?**

- **Under what circumstances do you feel you must agree with a person in order to accept them?**

- **When have you felt unaccepted, like you don't belong?**

Action steps:

- In light of our discussion, what is God asking you to do?

- How will you obey his prompting?

- When will you do it?

- Who will help you?

- With whom will you share what you have learned before we meet again?

II. Forgiving others and asking forgiveness

Key question: *Who do you need to forgive? Who do you need to ask for forgiveness?*

Part of living in a fallen world means we sin against one another and are sinned against. Sometimes it's unintentional, sometimes it's intentional, but either way it hurts. What then? We have a hard time letting go of offenses against us. We have a hard time acknowledging the harm we've done to others. The forgiveness that lies at the heart of the gospel is the only thing that has the power to free us to live authentically within imperfect relationships with imperfect people.

This forgiveness isn't cheap. It doesn't mean we pretend no real harm was done. It doesn't mean we pretend to forget. It means we remember, acknowledge the hurt, and choose to let go anyway. Only through the power of God can we access this kind of forgiveness: we forgive because he forgave us (Col. 3:13).

 Meditation

"Silence is sometimes the best answer."

— Dalai Lama XIVs

Remember that both parts of the forgiveness process are essential: we need to ask for forgiveness and we need to forgive others. One without the other is incomplete. When we confess our sins, do what we can to make it right, and embrace the fact that we are forgiven... only then are we truly free to forgive others and not hold onto grievances. If we can't forgive others, we've likely not accepted God's forgiveness for ourselves.

This week read and reflect daily on the scripture on the next page. Open a natural flow of conversational prayer with the Holy Spirit as you meditate on the scriptures, inviting him to reveal himself to you. Then gather with those who journey alongside you and interact over the discipleship questions.

Luke 15:11-32

To illustrate the point further, Jesus told them this story: "A man had two sons. 12 The younger son told his father, 'I want my share of your estate now before you die.' So his father agreed to divide his wealth between his sons.

13 "A few days later this younger son packed all his belongings and moved to a distant land, and there he wasted all his money in wild living. 14 About the time his money ran out, a great famine swept over the land, and he began to starve. 15 He persuaded a local farmer to hire him, and the man sent him into his fields to feed the pigs. 16 The young man became so hungry that even the pods he was feeding the pigs looked good to him. But no one gave him anything.

17 "When he finally came to his senses, he said to himself, 'At home even the hired servants have food enough to spare, and here I am dying of hunger! 18 I will go home to my father and say, "Father, I have sinned against both heaven and you, 19 and I am no longer worthy of being called your son. Please take me on as a hired servant."'

20 "So he returned home to his father. And while he was still a long way off, his father saw him coming. Filled with love and compassion, he ran to his son, embraced him, and kissed him. 21 His son said to him, 'Father, I have sinned against both heaven and you, and I am no longer worthy of being called your son.'

22 "But his father said to the servants, 'Quick! Bring the finest robe in the house and put it on him. Get a ring for his finger and sandals for his feet. 23 And kill the calf we have been fattening. We must celebrate with a feast, 24 for this son of mine was dead and has now returned to life. He was lost, but now he is found.' So the party began.

25 "Meanwhile, the older son was in the fields working. When he returned home, he heard music and dancing in the house, 26 and he asked one of the servants what was going on. 27 'Your brother is back,' he was told, 'and your father has killed the fattened calf. We are celebrating because of his safe return.'

28 "The older brother was angry and wouldn't go in. His father came out and begged him, 29 but he replied, 'All these years I've slaved for you and never once refused to do a single thing you told me to. And in all that time you never gave me even one young goat for a feast with my friends.

30 Yet when this son of yours comes back after squandering your money on prostitutes, you celebrate by killing the fattened calf!'

31 "His father said to him, 'Look, dear son, you have always stayed by me, and everything I have is yours. 32 We had to celebrate this happy day. For your brother was dead and has come back to life! He was lost, but now he is found!'"

Matthew 6:14-15

"If you forgive those who sin against you, your heavenly Father will forgive you. 15 But if you refuse to forgive others, your Father will not forgive your sins."

Discipleship questions:

- **When is the last time you asked for forgiveness?**

- **When is the last time you asked for help with something you couldn't do on your own?**

- **What does it usually take to bring you to the point of asking for forgiveness? For help?**

- **What emotions surround that process?**

- **What response do you expect from others? What leads you to expect that response?**

Meditation

"Always forgive your enemies; nothing annoys them so much."

— Oscar Wilde

Forgiveness inventory

Write down wrongs you've done and wrongs that have been done to you on scraps of paper. Then, one by one, throw those scraps of paper into a bonfire.

Action steps:

- **In light of our discussion, what is God asking you to do?**

- **How will you obey his prompting?**

- **When will you do it?**

- **Who will help you?**

- **With whom will you share what you have learned before we meet again?**

III. Confronting each other with humility when necessary

Key question: *How are you being honest with those around you and confronting when necessary?*

God requires that we look honestly at ourselves and at where we fall short. For a faith that places such emphasis on repentance, this should not be so difficult for Christians, but it invariably is. We will sometimes go to great lengths to avoid looking ourselves in the mirror.

For that reason we need one another. Confronting others is not an enviable job, as any prophet can attest. But it is a necessary one. Sometimes God uses other believers to point out where we are failing and how we need to change. For this reason, we need to be willing to confront one another honestly when it is necessary, even if it means we risk others being angry with us.

Meditation

"Remember that the best relationship is one in which your love for each other exceeds your need for each other."

— **Dalai Lama XIV**

At the same time we need to act and speak from a place of humility. We are no better than others, even when we need to point out a fault. Let us avoid the trap of the Pharisees.

This week read and reflect daily on the scripture below. Open a natural flow of conversational prayer with the Holy Spirit as you meditate on the scriptures, inviting him to reveal himself to you. Then gather with those who journey alongside you and interact over the discipleship questions.

2 Samuel 12:1-13

> *So the Lord sent Nathan the prophet to tell David this story: "There were two men in a certain town. One was rich, and one was poor. 2 The rich man owned a great many sheep and cattle.*

3 The poor man owned nothing but one little lamb he had bought. He raised that little lamb, and it grew up with his children. It ate from the man's own plate and drank from his cup. He cuddled it in his arms like a baby daughter. 4 One day a guest arrived at the home of the rich man. But instead of killing an animal from his own flock or herd, he took the poor man's lamb and killed it and prepared it for his guest."

5 David was furious. "As surely as the Lord lives," he vowed, "any man who would do such a thing deserves to die! 6 He must repay four lambs to the poor man for the one he stole and for having no pity."

7 Then Nathan said to David, "You are that man! The Lord, the God of Israel, says: I anointed you king of Israel and saved you from the power of Saul. 8 I gave you your master's house and his wives and the kingdoms of Israel and Judah. And if that had not been enough, I would have given you much, much more. 9 Why, then, have you despised the word of the Lord and done this horrible deed? For you have murdered Uriah the Hittite with the sword of the Ammonites and stolen his wife. 10 From this time on, your family will live by the sword because you have despised me by taking Uriah's wife to be your own.

11 "This is what the Lord says: Because of what you have done, I will cause your own household to rebel against you. I will give your wives to another man before your very eyes, and he will go to bed with them in public view. 12 You did it secretly, but I will make this happen to you openly in the sight of all Israel."

13 Then David confessed to Nathan, "I have sinned against the Lord."

Galatians 2:11-14

But when Peter came to Antioch, I had to oppose him to his face, for what he did was very wrong. 12 When he first arrived, he ate with the Gentile believers, who were not circumcised. But afterward, when some friends of James came, Peter wouldn't eat with the Gentiles anymore. He was afraid of criticism from these people who insisted on the necessity of circumcision. 13 As a result, other Jewish believers followed Peter's hypocrisy, and even Barnabas was led astray by their hypocrisy.

14 When I saw that they were not following the truth of the gospel message, I said to Peter in front of all the others, "Since you, a Jew by birth, have discarded the Jewish laws and are living like a Gentile, why are you now trying to make these Gentiles follow the Jewish traditions?

Easy or hard?

Some people find it easy to confront others. Some find it difficult. Generally speaking, those who find it difficult need to speak out more often. Those who find it easy need to speak out less often. Which camp do you fall into? What might you do to make the necessary changes in how you confront?

Discipleship questions:

- When have you sensed the need to confront someone? What did you do? What was the result?

- When is a time someone confronted you? How did that feel? What can you learn from that experience about confronting others?

- Do you find it difficult or easy to confront someone? Explain.

- How do you go about examining your heart and motives before talking with someone? What might a good process look like?

Action steps:

- **In light of our discussion, what is God asking you to do?**

- **How will you obey his prompting?**

- **When will you do it?**

- **Who will help you?**

- **With whom will you share what you have learned before we meet again?**

IV. Praying for and with others

Key question: *How are you praying for and with others?*

Our relationships have been described as horizontal and vertical: our horizontal relationships with one another and our vertical relationship with God. In prayer, we bring those two categories of relationships together. We pray for those we are in horizontal relationship with... bringing their needs and concerns before God. We pray with others to God... bringing them into our relationship with God. That creates a relational intimacy that calls for nothing less than full authenticity—with both God and others. At the same time, our relationship with God is enriched by our relationships with others. And our relationships with others are enriched by our relationship with God.

 Meditation

"The Bible tells us to love our neighbors, and also to love our enemies; probably because generally they are the same people."

— **G.K. Chesterton**

This week read and reflect daily on the scripture below. Open a natural flow of conversational prayer with the Holy Spirit as you meditate on the scriptures, inviting him to reveal himself to you. Then gather with those who journey alongside you and interact over the discipleship questions.

Colossians 1:3-14

> *We always pray for you, and we give thanks to God, the Father of our Lord Jesus Christ. 4 For we have heard of your faith in Christ Jesus and your love for all of God's people, 5 which come from your confident hope of what God has reserved for you in heaven. You have had this expectation ever since you first heard the truth of the Good News.*

> *6 This same Good News that came to you is going out all over the world. It is bearing fruit everywhere by changing lives, just as it changed your lives from the day you first heard and understood the truth about God's wonderful grace.*

7 You learned about the Good News from Epaphras, our beloved co-worker. He is Christ's faithful servant, and he is helping us on your behalf. 8 He has told us about the love for others that the Holy Spirit has given you.

9 So we have not stopped praying for you since we first heard about you. We ask God to give you complete knowledge of his will and to give you spiritual wisdom and understanding. 10 Then the way you live will always honor and please the Lord, and your lives will produce every kind of good fruit. All the while, you will grow as you learn to know God better and better.

11 We also pray that you will be strengthened with all his glorious power so you will have all the endurance and patience you need. May you be filled with joy, 12 always thanking the Father. He has enabled you to share in the inheritance that belongs to his people, who live in the light. 13 For he has rescued us from the kingdom of darkness and transferred us into the Kingdom of his dear Son, 14 who purchased our freedom and forgave our sins.

Praying the Lord's prayer

One way to structure our prayers so we're praying in alignment with the teachings of Jesus is to pray through the Lord's prayer. It's not the only pattern for prayer, but it is a good one.

Matthew 6:9-13

Pray like this:

Our Father in heaven,
may your name be kept holy.
(Prayer of recognition of who God is)

10 May your Kingdom come soon.
(Prayer of hope for the future)

May your will be done on earth,
as it is in heaven.
(Prayer of alignment with God's will)

11 Give us today the food we need,
(Prayer for the provision of needs)

12 and forgive us our sins,
as we have forgiven those who sin against us.
(Prayer for forgiveness)

13 And don't let us yield to temptation,
but rescue us from the evil one.
(Prayer for protection against temptation)

Discipleship questions:

- **Who or what do you feel compelled to pray for regularly?**

- **How often do you pray corporately with others? In what settings?**

- **What time do you have set-aside to pray individually?**

- **What settings are most conducive to prayer for you?**

- **What are some creative ways you can branch out in your prayers?**

Prayer exercise:

Pray in some different places and at different times than you normally do this week. If you usually pray in the morning, try praying at night. If you usually pray alone in silence, pray as you walk or run around the neighborhood. What other changes do you notice when you pray in different places and at different times?

Action steps:

- **In light of our discussion, what is God asking you to do?**

- **How will you obey his prompting?**

- **When will you do it?**

- **Who will help you?**

- **With whom will you share what you have learned before we meet again?**

Guide for Discipling

V. Supporting each other honestly through life challenges

Key question: *How are you supporting others honestly through life challenges?*

People facing challenges are all around us. Being generous relationally is one of the most significant contributions we can make. As we relationally invest in others, we—as well as they— are transformed.

How did God invest in us? In a very personal, relational way. Jesus came down as one of us. He invested in long-term relationships. He took our place on the cross. God the Father saw to the most intimate details of our creation, making us who he wanted us to be. The Holy Spirit lives within us, providing constant divine communication and direction. All of that required a lot more investment than writing a check and saying, "Be warm and well-fed." He warmed and fed us himself.

In the same way, we are to invest in other people to the degree that we are able. God placed the people who are in our lives there for a reason. We are to love them and reflect God to them. We are there to meet their needs. Yes, we only have so much relational capacity. We can only know so many people on a personal level. How are we investing the relational capacity we do have? The degree to which we do that reflects a life of generosity.

 Meditation

"In misfortune, which friend remains a friend?"

— Euripides

This week read and reflect daily on the scripture on the next page. Open a natural flow of conversational prayer with the Holy Spirit as you meditate on the scriptures, inviting him to reveal himself to you. Then gather with those who journey alongside you and interact over the discipleship questions.

1 Thessalonians 2:8-13

We loved you so much that we shared with you not only God's Good News but our own lives, too. 9 Don't you remember, dear brothers and sisters, how hard we worked among you? Night and day we toiled to earn a living so that we would not be a burden to any of you as we preached God's Good News to you. 10 You yourselves are our witnesses—and so is God—that we were devout and honest and faultless toward all of you believers. 11 And you know that we treated each of you as a father treats his own children. 12 We pleaded with you, encouraged you, and urged you to live your lives in a way that God would consider worthy. For he called you to share in his Kingdom and glory.

13 Therefore, we never stop thanking God that when you received his message from us, you didn't think of our words as mere human ideas. You accepted what we said as the very word of God—which, of course, it is. And this word continues to work in you who believe.

John 15:9-17

"I have loved you even as the Father has loved me. Remain in my love. 10 When you obey my commandments, you remain in my love, just as I obey my Father's commandments and remain in his love. 11 I have told you these things so that you will be filled with my joy. Yes, your joy will overflow! 12 This is my commandment: Love each other in the same way I have loved you. 13 There is no greater love than to lay down one's life for one's friends. 14 You are my friends if you do what I command. 15 I no longer call you slaves, because a master doesn't confide in his slaves. Now you are my friends, since I have told you everything the Father told me. 16 You didn't choose me. I chose you. I appointed you to go and produce lasting fruit, so that the Father will give you whatever you ask for, using my name. 17 This is my command: Love each other.

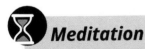 **Meditation**

"Be yourself; everyone else is already taken."

— Oscar Wilde

Discipleship questions:

- With whom are you in regular relationship?

- How would you describe those relationships? Do you tend to be giving more or receiving more?

- What are some ways you could give to those you are in relationship with?

- What expectations do you have of others that make it difficult for you to invest in them?

- What are some of the ways people have invested in you over the course of your life?

- What impact did that have? What are some of the ways God has invested in you?

Action steps:

- **In light of our discussion, what is God asking you to do?**

- **How will you obey his prompting?**

- **When will you do it?**

- **Who will help you?**

- **With whom will you share what you have learned before we meet again?**

Community Transformation

Personal involvement with others to facilitate positive change where you live and beyond

I. Participating in a faith community that reaches outside of itself

Key question: *How is your faith community reaching outside of itself?*

The seeds of world transformation are found in the faith community—not only in we who have the Spirit living within us, but in others who are being redeemed, joining our faith communities, and starting new ones. Like yeast working into dough, a little bit goes a long way and it spreads throughout. That's how the Kingdom of God grows. Sprinkle in a few communities of faith, and they work their way through the whole broader community.

In this sense, individual faith communities are not the ends, but the means. They are not the goal in and of themselves. They are the tool God uses to create wider transformational change throughout the world. Through the actions of a faith community, things change and people hear. We see illustrations of how this works throughout the book of Acts.

Meditation

"I alone cannot change the world, but I can cast a stone across the waters to create many ripples."

— **Mother Teresa**

Consider what your faith community is doing to reach outside itself and bring transformation to the world around you. You as an individual cannot do this alone. However, if your faith community is not engaged in reaching out, it is your responsibility to bring the issue to the fore. Ask those in leadership how you can be part of something bigger together.

This week read and reflect daily on the scripture on the next page. Open a natural flow of conversational prayer with the Holy Spirit as you meditate on the scriptures, inviting him to reveal himself to you. Then gather with those who journey alongside you and interact over the discipleship questions.

Luke 13:20-21

He also asked, "What else is the Kingdom of God like? 21 It is like the yeast a woman used in making bread. Even though she put only a little yeast in three measures of flour, it permeated every part of the dough."

Acts 13:38-49

"Brothers, listen! We are here to proclaim that through this man Jesus there is forgiveness for your sins. 39 Everyone who believes in him is declared right with God—something the law of Moses could never do. 40 Be careful! Don't let the prophets' words apply to you. For they said,

41 'Look, you mockers,
  be amazed and die!
For I am doing something in your own day,
  something you wouldn't believe
  even if someone told you about it.'"42 As Paul and Barnabas left the synagogue that day, the people begged them to speak about these things again the next week. 43 Many Jews and devout converts to Judaism followed Paul and Barnabas, and the two men urged them to continue to rely on the grace of God.

44 The following week almost the entire city turned out to hear them preach the word of the Lord. 45 But when some of the Jews saw the crowds, they were jealous; so they slandered Paul and argued against whatever he said.

46 Then Paul and Barnabas spoke out boldly and declared, "It was necessary that we first preach the word of God to you Jews. But since you have rejected it and judged yourselves unworthy of eternal life, we will offer it to the Gentiles. 47 For the Lord gave us this command when he said,

'I have made you a light to the Gentiles,
  to bring salvation to the farthest corners of the earth.'"

48 When the Gentiles heard this, they were very glad and thanked the Lord for his message; and all who were chosen for eternal life became believers. 49 So the Lord's message spread throughout that region.

Acts 4:32-35

All the believers were united in heart and mind. And they felt that what they owned was not their own, so they shared everything they had. 33 The apostles testified powerfully to the resurrection of the Lord Jesus, and God's great blessing was upon them all. 34 There were no needy people among them, because those who owned land or houses would sell them 35 and bring the money to the apostles to give to those in need.

Zephaniah 3:9

"Then I will purify the lips of the peoples,
   that all of them may call on the name of the Lord
   and serve him shoulder to shoulder." (NIV)

Discipleship questions:

- How can your faith community mirror the love of God to the broader community around you? When people look at your community from the outside, what do they see?

- How could you work together with others to serve more effectively than you could alone?

- Who might you need to work alongside?

- How can you serve in ways that bring widespread change to the larger community?

- What effects would you like to see result from your ministry? Describe the vision.

Community Ministry Analysis:

In your group, determine major needs in your local community. Then rank the needs in terms of which ones are most pressing. Determine how your faith community can strategically respond to those needs.

Action steps:

- **In light of our discussion, what is God asking you to do?**

- **How will you obey his prompting?**

- **When will you do it?**

- **Who will help you?**

- **With whom will you share what you have learned before we meet again?**

II. Praying for healing and reconciliation in society

Key question: *How are you praying for healing and reconciliation in society?*

We live in a society in dire need of healing. Our world is divided against itself by race, by class, by ethnic group, by religion. Sin separates us not only from God but from one another. We are a world and a people in need of healing.

Coming face to face with the needs around us for healing and reconciliation brings us face to face with our own sense of inadequacy. We know we are not strong enough, rich enough, smart enough, powerful enough to solve people's problems. We are not God; we can only do so much. That's why we bring these needs before him in prayer. We alone cannot bring healing and reconciliation, but we can experience the power of God working through us as we rely on him and listen to his voice and direction.

Meditation

"Forgiving and being reconciled to our enemies or our loved ones are not about pretending that things are other than they are. It is not about patting one another on the back and turning a blind eye to the wrong. True reconciliation exposes the awfulness, the abuse, the hurt, the truth. It could even sometimes make things worse. It is a risky undertaking but in the end it is worthwhile, because in the end only an honest confrontation with reality can bring real healing. Superficial reconciliation can bring only superficial healing."

— **Desmond Tutu**

Prayer

Ask God to break your heart over the things that break his heart. Ask him to bring about healing and reconciliation. Ask God to show you where he is at work.

This week read and reflect daily on the scripture below. Open a natural flow of conversational prayer with the Holy Spirit as you meditate on the scriptures, inviting him to reveal himself to you. Then gather with those who journey alongside you and interact over the discipleship questions.

Luke 15:11-32

To illustrate the point further, Jesus told them this story: "A man had two sons. 12 The younger son told his father, 'I want my share of your estate now before you die.' So his father agreed to divide his wealth between his sons.

13 "A few days later this younger son packed all his belongings and moved to a distant land, and there he wasted all his money in wild living. 14 About the time his money ran out, a great famine swept over the land, and he began to starve. 15 He persuaded a local farmer to hire him, and the man sent him into his fields to feed the pigs. 16 The young man became so hungry that even the pods he was feeding the pigs looked good to him. But no one gave him anything.

17 "When he finally came to his senses, he said to himself, 'At home even the hired servants have food enough to spare, and here I am dying of hunger! 18 I will go home to my father and say, "Father, I have sinned against both heaven and you, 19 and I am no longer worthy of being called your son. Please take me on as a hired servant."'

20 "So he returned home to his father. And while he was still a long way off, his father saw him coming. Filled with love and compassion, he ran to his son, embraced him, and kissed him. 21 His son said to him, 'Father, I have sinned against both heaven and you, and I am no longer worthy of being called your son.'

22 "But his father said to the servants, 'Quick! Bring the finest robe in the house and put it on him. Get a ring for his finger and sandals for his feet. 23 And kill the calf we have been fattening. We must celebrate with a feast, 24 for this son of mine was dead and has now returned to life. He was lost, but now he is found.' So the party began.

25 "Meanwhile, the older son was in the fields working. When he returned home, he heard music and dancing in the house, 26 and he asked one of the servants what was going on. 27 'Your brother is back,' he was told, 'and your father has killed the fattened calf. We are celebrating because of his safe return.'

28 "The older brother was angry and wouldn't go in. His father came out and begged him,

29 but he replied, 'All these years I've slaved for you and never once refused to do a single thing you told me to. And in all that time you never gave me even one young goat for a feast with my friends. 30 Yet when this son of yours comes back after squandering your money on prostitutes, you celebrate by killing the fattened calf!'

31 "His father said to him, 'Look, dear son, you have always stayed by me, and everything I have is yours. 32 We had to celebrate this happy day. For your brother was dead and has come back to life! He was lost, but now he is found!'"

Matthew 15:29-31

Jesus returned to the Sea of Galilee and climbed a hill and sat down. 30 A vast crowd brought to him people who were lame, blind, crippled, those who couldn't speak, and many others. They laid them before Jesus, and he healed them all. 31 The crowd was amazed! Those who hadn't been able to speak were talking, the crippled were made well, the lame were walking, and the blind could see again! And they praised the God of Israel.

Mark 9:28-29

Afterward, when Jesus was alone in the house with his disciples, they asked him, "Why couldn't we cast out that evil spirit?"

29 Jesus replied, "This kind can be cast out only by prayer."

Meditation

"When we honestly ask ourselves which person in our lives mean the most to us, we often find that it is those who, instead of giving advice, solutions, or cures, have chosen rather to share our pain and touch our wounds with a warm and tender hand. The friend who can be silent with us in a moment of despair or confusion, who can stay with us in an hour of grief and bereavement, who can tolerate not knowing, not curing, not healing and face with us the reality of our powerlessness, that is a friend who cares."

— **Henri J.M. Nouwen,** *Out of Solitude*

Discipleship questions:

- Where do you see the need for reconciliation?

- Where do you see the need for healing?

- How are you praying for these things? For what are you asking God?

- Where do you see God at work?

- Into what situations or relationships can you bring some level of healing or reconciliation?

Action steps:

- In light of our discussion, what is God asking you to do?

- How will you obey his prompting?

- When will you do it?

- Who will help you?

- With whom will you share what you have learned before we meet again?

III. Involving yourself in social justice needs in the broader community

Key question: *How are you involved in social justice needs within your community?*

In many churches, talk of social justice issues makes people afraid that the gospel message is being lost and the church is becoming too "liberal." Although it's true that some churches have substituted a social gospel for a literal one, a look at scripture makes clear that God has always intended social justice to be an outworking of the gospel of Jesus. They go together.

A church, acting as the church is supposed to act, will serve the cause of justice, speaking up for the widow and the orphan and those that cannot speak up for themselves. What is your part in that? Are you a passive individual allowing others in the church to act on your behalf? Or are you willing to step out personally as part of a broader effort? When you do, very often, you will find God is already there ahead of you. You are simply participating in what he is already doing.

 Meditation

"God is in the slums, in the cardboard boxes where the poor play house. God is in the silence of a mother who has infected her child with a virus that will end both their lives. God is in the cries heard under the rubble of war. God is in the debris of wasted opportunity and lives, and God is with us if we are with them."
— **Bono, National Prayer Breakfast 2006**

 Meditation

"Don't let what you cannot do interfere with what you can do."
— **John Wooden**

This week read and reflect daily on the scripture below. Open a natural flow of conversational prayer with the Holy Spirit as you meditate on the scriptures, inviting him to reveal himself to you. Then gather with those who journey alongside you and interact over the discipleship questions.

> **Exercise:**
>
> Once you've identified a particular problem in your community to address, gather together and spend some time in prayer listening to God and trying to brainstorm some possible solutions. Think how you can act both individually and corporately.

Micah 6:8

> No, O people, the Lord has told you what is good,
>   and this is what he requires of you:
> to do what is right, to love mercy,
>   and to walk humbly with your God.

Isaiah 61:1-3

> The Spirit of the Sovereign Lord is upon me,
>   for the Lord has anointed me
>   to bring good news to the poor.
> He has sent me to comfort the brokenhearted
>   and to proclaim that captives will be released
>   and prisoners will be freed.
> 2 He has sent me to tell those who mourn
>   that the time of the Lord's favor has come,
>   and with it, the day of God's anger against their enemies.
> 3 To all who mourn in Israel,
>   he will give a crown of beauty for ashes,
> a joyous blessing instead of mourning,
>   festive praise instead of despair.
> In their righteousness, they will be like great oaks
>   that the Lord has planted for his own glory.

Discipleship questions:

- **What injustices do you feel most keenly?**

- **What can you do about them?**

- **What risk might that involve for you personally?**

- **What rewards might there be?**

- **What historical figures do you most admire for the ways in which they stood in the way of injustice? How could you emulate them?**

- **How can you work together with others in your faith community to make a difference?**

Journal:

Who are the poor in your community? Write about them. What qualities do they share? What challenges do they face? What needs do they have?

Action steps:

- **In light of our discussion, what is God asking you to do?**

- **How will you obey his prompting?**

- **When will you do it?**

- **Who will help you?**

- **With whom will you share what you have learned before we meet again?**

IV. Caring for God's creation in practical ways

Key question: *How are you caring for God's creation?*

Sometimes followers of Jesus have believed—wrongly—that they do not need to care for the environment because God will destroy the world anyway at the second coming. When we look at scripture, we are told to care for and oversee creation. In Eden he told us to tend the animals, the plants, the land. We are responsible.

When Jesus returns, he returns to redeem not only us but all of creation. The scripture passages in this section clarify the extent of his restoration and our role in it. When we care for creation and participate in its restoration, we experience God and are taking a role in the coming Kingdom of God.

Meditation

"If your daily life seems poor, do not blame it; blame yourself, tell yourself that you are not poet enough to call forth its riches; for to the creator there is no poverty and no poor indifferent place."

— Rainer Maria Rilke

Even now, there are practical things we can do to care for creation. Caring for animals, working to alleviate animal suffering, growing food, replenishing tired soil, picking up trash, recycling, planting trees…. Brainstorm together to think of more.

This week read and reflect daily on the scripture below. Open a natural flow of conversational prayer with the Holy Spirit as you meditate on the scriptures, inviting him to reveal himself to you. Then gather with those who journey alongside you and interact over the discipleship questions.

Genesis 1:31

> *Then God looked over all he had made, and he saw that it was very good!*

Genesis 2:15

> *The Lord God placed the man in the Garden of Eden to tend and watch over it.*

Guide for Discipling

Genesis 3:17-19

And to the man he said,

"Since you listened to your wife and ate from the tree
whose fruit I commanded you not to eat,
the ground is cursed because of you.
All your life you will struggle to scratch a living from it.
18 It will grow thorns and thistles for you,
though you will eat of its grains.19 By the sweat of your brow
will you have food to eat
until you return to the ground
from which you were made.
For you were made from dust,
and to dust you will return."

Romans 8:19-23

For all creation is waiting eagerly for that future day when God will reveal who his children really are. 20 Against its will, all creation was subjected to God's curse. But with eager hope, 21 the creation looks forward to the day when it will join God's children in glorious freedom from death and decay. 22 For we know that all creation has been groaning as in the pains of childbirth right up to the present time. 23 And we believers also groan, even though we have the Holy Spirit within us as a foretaste of future glory, for we long for our bodies to be released from sin and suffering.

2 Chronicles 7:14

Then if my people who are called by my name will humble themselves and pray and seek my face and turn from their wicked ways, I will hear from heaven and will forgive their sins and restore their land.

Imagine...

... creation restored and no longer crying out for redemption

... the people of God hiring the poor to heal their own environments (www. edenprojects.org)

... the impact of that hiring on the local economy (www.edenprojects.org)

... the end of deforestation, erosion and soil depletion

... productive agriculture restored to local farmers

... no more endangered or extinct animal species

... long-term sustainability

Discipleship questions:

- How do you think God has called us to steward his creation?

- How was our relationship with the earth damaged by the fall?

- In 2 Chronicles 7:14, what did God mean by healing the land? Why did the land need to be healed?

- Where do you sense the creation groaning?

- What can you do—along with your faith community—to participate in caring for creation?

- Brainstorm some small, practical ways to participate in transforming creation. Think both locally and globally.

Action steps:

- **In light of our discussion, what is God asking you to do?**

- **How will you obey his prompting?**

- **When will you do it?**

- **Who will help you?**

- **With whom will you share what you have learned before we meet again?**

V. Helping others create healthy lives and relationships

Key question: *How are you helping others promote healthy lives and relationships?*

It's not only creation that needs to be redeemed and transformed—it's us as well. We need to help people rid their lives of destructive behaviors and patterns and replace them with healthy ones. In fact, if we focus only on ridding of destructive behavior and don't try to replace it with anything, we create a void that invites new kinds of destructive behavior. The cycle of destruction isn't broken just when we stop destroying things—it's broken when we start building things.

We need to promote health both on an individual level and on a community-wide level. Just as an individual might replace a pattern of gossip with healthy listening skills, consider what we can put in place of destruction on a community-wide scale: community centers instead of gangs, education instead of ignorance, work instead of idleness. When more and more people begin making these kinds of positive changes, we'll see whole communities growing toward greater health. Consider how your faith community can band together to see some of this vision become a reality.

Meditation

"There is a God-shaped vacuum in the heart of every person, and it can never be filled by any created thing. It can only be filled by God, made known through Jesus Christ."

— **Blaise Pascal, *Pensées***

This week read and reflect daily on the scripture that follow. Open a natural flow of conversational prayer with the Holy Spirit as you meditate on the scriptures, inviting him to reveal himself to you. Then gather with those who journey alongside you and interact over the discipleship questions.

Ephesians 4:17-32

With the Lord's authority I say this: Live no longer as the Gentiles do, for they are hopelessly confused. 18 Their minds are full of darkness; they wander far from the life God gives because they have closed their minds and hardened their hearts against him. 19 They have no sense of shame. They live for lustful pleasure and eagerly practice every kind of impurity.

20 But that isn't what you learned about Christ. 21 Since you have heard about Jesus and have learned the truth that comes from him, 22 throw off your old sinful nature and your former way of life, which is corrupted by lust and deception. 23 Instead, let the Spirit renew your thoughts and attitudes. 24 Put on your new nature, created to be like God—truly righteous and holy.

25 So stop telling lies. Let us tell our neighbors the truth, for we are all parts of the same body. 26 And "don't sin by letting anger control you." Don't let the sun go down while you are still angry, 27 for anger gives a foothold to the devil.

28 If you are a thief, quit stealing. Instead, use your hands for good hard work, and then give generously to others in need. 29 Don't use foul or abusive language. Let everything you say be good and helpful, so that your words will be an encouragement to those who hear them.

30 And do not bring sorrow to God's Holy Spirit by the way you live. Remember, he has identified you as his own, guaranteeing that you will be saved on the day of redemption.

31 Get rid of all bitterness, rage, anger, harsh words, and slander, as well as all types of evil behavior. 32 Instead, be kind to each other, tenderhearted, forgiving one another, just as God through Christ has forgiven you.

John 10:10

The thief comes only to steal and kill and destroy; I have come that they may have life, and have it to the full. (NIV)

Prayer and reflection:

Spend some time envisioning the kind of community God could transform this community into. What would that look like?

Discipleship questions:

- What are you sensing from God about your community?

- What do you see in your community that needs change?

- With what could you fill the voids that would be left?

- Who might help you do that?

- How might your faith community join you in that? How might you join your faith community in that?

Action steps:

- **In light of our discussion, what is God asking you to do?**

- **How will you obey his prompting?**

- **When will you do it?**

- **Who will help you?**

- **With whom will you share what you have learned before we meet again?**

What's next?

It's up to you to do some listening to the Holy Spirit. Take a look at the big picture and decide where God is leading you next. With a holistic system, it's always a surprise. No matter what area of life God directs you to dig into next, continue to engage in an ongoing action-reflection process as you live out your faith.

About the Authors

Dr. Robert E. Logan has worked in full-time ministry for over thirty years as a church planter, pastor, missions leader, consultant, and ministry coach. He is internationally recognized as an authority in church planting, church growth and leadership development. Bob invests his life to equip people to be the hands, feet, and voice of Jesus to make disciples and multiply churches.

Dr. Charles R. Ridley has utilized his expertise in the area of measurement and assessment in the development of the church planter profile, which has shaped the foundation of church-planter selection all over the world. He has also done extensive work on coach competencies and assessments, conducting a qualitative international research project. A licensed psychologist and professor at Texas A&M University, Chuck earned his PhD in counseling psychology from the University of Minnesota.

About Logan Leadership

Our vision is every person living, growing and multiplying together as disciples of Jesus who demonstrate the Kingdom of God among all peoples.

Our mission is catalyzing leaders to accelerate their movement toward this vision.

Our approach integrates biblical principles with social science insights by helping leaders...

- **sharpen thinking skills**
- **focus actions**
- **contextualize solutions**
- **create reproducible processes**
- **increase ministry capacity**

Find out more about us at http://loganleadership.com.

Appendix

Love God | Love Others | Make Disciples

Logan Leadership is the central hub for information and resources to assist you in your personal growth and your ministry. With decades of experience coaching and consulting with leaders worldwide, our desire is to equip leaders to live, grow, and multiply together as disciples of Jesus who demonstrate the Kingdom of God among all peoples.

We're all about helping you get where you want to go. That looks different for each ministry or organization. Depending on your goals, we can provide targeted coaching, training, resource development, assessment, and/or consulting.

Over the years, we've helped hundreds of churches, denominations and mission organizations meet and exceed their goals. That can mean implementing discipleship processes, retooling leadership development, turning around congregations in decline, or any number of other aims.

Coaching — The accountability and clarity that coaching provides gives you the follow through you need to accomplish the goals you've set for yourself and your ministry.

Consulting — We can enter your ministry situation to help you find contextualized solutions for your specific needs.

Training — We design interactive training systems geared toward coaches, church planters, disciplers, pastors and key leaders.

Resource Development — We can create and/or adapt Logan Leadership resources that speak effectively and appropriately to the culture and people of your organization.

Assessments — Using God's Word and proven social science insights, we offer a number of effective assessment tools that help you and your organization make smart decisions.

Discipleship Resources

To fulfill the Great Commission, we must be faithful to make disciples of Jesus. Logan Leadership has created several resources to assist you in your personal discipleship journey and in encouraging others toward a closer walk with God.

Guides for Discipling (Digital) — Now that you have completed the Guide for Discipling, you may want to share some of the lessons contained herein with individuals or groups in your own ministry. The digital Guides for Discipling allow you to do that in an affordable, structured way. Available individually or as a set, the guides relate to the eight dimensions of a disciple of Jesus:

Experiencing God

Spiritual Responsiveness

Sacrificial Service

Generous Living

Disciplemaking

Personal Transformation

Authentic Relationships

Community Transformation

The digital Guides for Discipling are available at http://loganleadership.com.

The Discipleship Difference — Every person is different and we all reflect God in different ways. So why is our typical approach to discipleship the same across the board? The Discipleship Difference lays out an intentional, holistic, and relational approach to discipleship that is individualized to meet each person wherever they are.

The Discipleship Difference is available in print at http://amazon.com or at http://loganleadership.com.

Discipleship Cohort — How many years have you been trying to get discipleship going in your context? Are you willing to try something different? The Discipleship Cohort is a year-long cohort for implementing discipleship in your ministry context. Offered only once per year, this group is a deep dive into the eight dimensions of discipleship outlined in the companion book for this course, The Discipleship Difference. Check http://loganleadership.com for details on the next open application period.

Disciple Assessment — Your church will only grow as well as the disciples that you develop. How can you reliably measure discipleship progress? The portrait of Jesus in the four gospels serves as our guide. Disciples seek to live and love like Jesus. The Disciple Assessment provides a snapshot of where you are in 8 dimensions of a disciple of Jesus, and is appropriate for individuals, small groups, churches, and missional communities. Learn more at http://discipleassessment.com.